Charles Kingsley

The water of Life

And other Sermons

Charles Kingsley

The water of Life
And other Sermons

ISBN/EAN: 9783743350106

Manufactured in Europe, USA, Canada, Australia, Japa

Cover: Foto ©Lupo / pixelio.de

Manufactured and distributed by brebook publishing software (www.brebook.com)

Charles Kingsley

The water of Life

THE WATER OF LIFE,

AND OTHER SERMONS.

THE WATER OF LIFE

AND OTHER SERMONS

BY

CHARLES KINGSLEY

London
MACMILLAN AND CO.
AND NEW YORK
1891

The right of translation is reserved

First Edition (Fcap. 8vo), 1867, Second, 1872.
Reprinted 1873, 1875 (Ex. Fcap. 8vo), 1879 (Crown 8vo).
Reprinted 1881, 1885, 1890, 1891.

CONTENTS.

SERMON I.

THE WATER OF LIFE. (*Revelation* xxii. 17.)   Page 1

SERMON II.

THE PHYSICIAN'S CALLING. (*St. Matthew* ix. 35.)   14

SERMON III.

THE VICTORY OF LIFE. (*Isaiah* xxxviii. 18, 19.)   27

SERMON IV.

THE WAGES OF SIN. (*Romans* vi. 21-23.)   40

SERMON V.

NIGHT AND DAY. (*Romans* xiii. 12.)   56

SERMON VI.

THE SHAKING OF THE HEAVENS AND THE EARTH.
(*Hebrews* xii. 26-29.) . . 68

SERMON VII.

THE BATTLE OF LIFE. (*Galatians* v. 16, 17.). . 83

SERMON VIII.

FREE GRACE. (*Isaiah* lv. 1.) . . 90

SERMON IX.

EZEKIEL'S VISION. (*Ezekiel* i. 1, 26.) 98

SERMON X.

RUTH. (*Ruth* ii. 4.). 111

SERMON XI.

SOLOMON. (*Ecclesiastes* i. 12-14.) 123

SERMON XII.

PROGRESS. (*Ecclesiastes* vii. 10.)   134

SERMON XIII.

FAITH. (*Habakkuk* ii. 4.).   143

SERMON XIV.

THE GREAT COMMANDMENT. (*Matthew* xxii. 37, 38.)   153

SERMON XV.

THE EARTHQUAKE. (*Psalm* xlvi. 1, 2.)   164

SERMON XVI.

THE METEOR SHOWER. (*Matthew* x. 29, 30.) .   176

SERMON XVII.

CHOLERA, 1866. (*Luke* vii. 16.)   . . .   189

SERMON XVIII.

THE WICKED SERVANT. (*Matthew* xviii. 23.) .   203

SERMON XIX.

CIVILIZED BARBARISM. (*Matthew* ix. 12.)   213

SERMON XX.

THE GOD OF NATURE. (*Psalm* cxlvii. 7-9.)   233

SERMON I.

THE WATER OF LIFE.

(Preached at Westminster Abbey.)

REVELATION xxii. 17.

And the Spirit and the Bride say, Come. And let him that heareth say, Come. And let him that is athirst come. And whosoever will, let him take the water of life freely.

THIS text is its own witness. It needs no man to testify to its origin. Its own words show it to be inspired and divine.

But not from its mere poetic beauty, great as that is: greater than we, in this wet and cold climate, can see at the first glance. We must go to the far East and the far South to understand the images which were called up in the mind of an old Jew at the very name of wells and water-springs; and why the Scriptures speak of them as special gifts of God, life-giving and divine. We must have seen the treeless waste, the blazing sun, the sickening glare, the choking dust, the parched rocks, the distant mountains quivering as in the vapour of a furnace; we must have felt the lassitude of heat, the torment of thirst, ere we can welcome, as did those old Easterns, the well dug long ago by pious hands, whither the maidens come with their jars at eventide, when the stone is rolled away, to water the thirsty flocks; or the living fountain, under the shadow of a great rock in a weary land, with its grove of trees, where all the birds for many a mile flock in, and shake the copses with their song; its lawn of green, on which the long-dazzled eye rests with refreshment and delight; its brook, wandering away—perhaps to be lost soon in burning sand, but giving, as far as it flows, Life; a Water of Life to plant, to animal, and to man.

All these images, which we have to call up in our minds one by one, presented themselves to the mind of an Eastern, whether Jew or heathen, at once, as a well-known and daily scene; and made him feel, at the very mention of a water-spring, that the speaker was telling him of the good and beautiful gift of a beneficent Being.

And yet—so do extremes meet—like thoughts, though not like images, may be called up in our minds, here in the heart of London, in murky alleys and foul courts, where there is too often, as in the poet's rotting sea—

'Water, water, everywhere,
Yet not a drop to drink.'

And we may bless God—as the Easterns bless Him for the ancestors who digged their wells—for every pious soul who now erects a drinking-fountain; for he fulfils the letter as well as the spirit of Scripture, by offering to the bodies as well as the souls of men the Water of Life freely.

But the text speaks not of earthly water. No doubt the words 'Water of Life' have a spiritual and mystic meaning. Yet that alone does not prove the inspiration of the text. They had a spiritual and mystic meaning already among the heathens of the East—Greeks and barbarians alike.

The East—and indeed the West likewise—was haunted by dreams of a Water of Life, a Fount of Perpetual Youth, a Cup of Immortality: dreams at which only the shallow and the ignorant will smile; for what are they but tokens of man's right to Immortality,—of his instinct that he is not as the beasts,—that there is somewhat in him which ought not to die, which need not die, and yet which may die, and which perhaps deserves to die? How could it be kept alive? how strengthened and refreshed into perpetual youth?

And water—with its life-giving and refreshing powers, often with medicinal properties seemingly miraculous—what better symbol could be found for that which would keep off death? Perhaps there was some reality which answered the symbol, some actual Cup of Immortality, some actual Fount of Youth. But who could attain to them? Surely the gods hid their own special treasure from the grasp of man. Surely that Water of Life was to be sought for far away, amid trackless mountain-peaks, guarded by dragons and demons. That Fount of Youth must be hidden in the rich glades of some tropic forest. That Cup of Immortality must be earned by years, by ages, of superhuman penance and self torture. Certain of the old Jews, it is true, had had deeper and truer thoughts. Here and there a psalmist had said, 'With God is the well of Life;' or a prophet had cried, 'Ho, every one that thirsteth, come ye to the waters, and buy without money and without price!' But the Jews had utterly forgotten (if the mass of them ever understood) the meaning of the old revelations; and, above all, the Pharisees, the most religious among them. To their minds, it was only by a proud asceticism,—by being not as other men were; only by doing some good thing—by performing some extraordinary religious feat,—that man could earn eternal life. And bitter and deadly was their selfish wrath when they heard that the Water of Life was within all men's reach, then and for ever; that The Eternal Life was in that Christ who spoke to them; that He gave it freely to whomsoever He would;—bitter their wrath when they heard His disciples declare that God had given to men Eternal Life; that the Spirit and the Bride said, Come.

They had, indeed, a graceful ceremony, handed down

to them from better times, as a sign that those words of the old psalmists and prophets had once meant something. At the Feast of Tabernacles—the harvest feast—at which God was especially to be thanked as the giver of fertility and Life, their priests drew water with great pomp from the pool of Siloam; connecting it with the words of the prophet: 'With joy shall ye draw water out of the wells of salvation.' But the ceremony had lost its meaning. It had become mechanical and empty. They had forgotten that God was a giver. They would have confessed, of course, that He was the Lord of Life : but they expected Him to prove that, not by giving Life, but by taking it away : not by saving the many, but by destroying all except a favoured few. But bitter and deadly was their wrath when they were told that their ceremony had still a living meaning, and a meaning not only for them, but for all men; for that mob of common people whom they looked on as accursed, because they knew not the law. Bitter and deadly was their selfish wrath, when they heard One who ate and drank with publicans and sinners stand up in the very midst of that grand ceremony, and cry; 'If any man thirst, let him come to Me and drink. He that believeth on Me, as the scripture hath said, Out of him shall flow rivers of living water.' A God who said to all 'Come,' was not the God they desired to rule over them. And thus the very words which prove the text to be divine and inspired, were marked out as such by those bigots of the old world, who in them saw and hated both Christ and His Father.

The Spirit and the Bride say, Come. Come, and drink freely.

Those words prove the text, and other texts like it in Holy Scripture, to be an utterly new Gospel and good news; an utterly new revelation and unveiling of God, and of the relations of God to man.

For the old legends and dreams, in whatsoever they differed, agreed at least in this, that the Water of Life was far away; infinitely difficult to reach; the prize only of some extraordinary favourite of fortune, or of some being of superhuman energy and endurance. The gods grudged life to mortals, as they grudged them joy and all good things. That God should say Come; that the Water of Life could be a gift, a grace, a boon of free generosity and perfect condescension, never entered into their minds. That the gods should keep their immortality to themselves seemed reasonable enough. That they should bestow it on a few heroes; and, far away above the stars, give them to eat of their ambrosia, and drink of their nectar, and so live for ever; that seemed reasonable enough likewise.

But that the God of gods, the Maker of the universe should say, 'Come, and drink freely;' that He should stoop from heaven to bring life and immortality to light,—to tell men what the Water of Life was, and where it was, and how to attain it; much more, that that God should stoop to become incarnate, and suffer and die on the cross, that He might purchase the Water of Life, not for a favoured few, but for all mankind; that He should offer it to all, without condition, stint, or drawback;—this, this, never entered into their wildest dreams.

And yet, when the strange news was told, it looked so probable, although so strange, to thousands who had seemed mere profligates or outcasts; it agreed so fully with the deepest voices of their own hearts, —with their thirst for a nobler, purer, more enduring Life,—with their highest idea of what a perfect God should be, if He meant to show His perfect goodness; it seemed at once so human and humane, and yet so superhuman and divine;—that they accepted it unhesitatingly, as a voice from God Himself, a revelation of the Eternal Author of the universe; as, God grant you may accept it this day.

And what is Life? And what is the Water of Life?

What are they indeed, my friends? You will find many answers to that question, in this, as in all ages: but the one which Scripture gives is this. Life is none other, according to the Scripture, than God Himself, Jesus Christ our Lord, who bestows on man His own

Spirit, to form in him His own character, which is the character of God.

He is The one Eternal Life; and it has been manifested in human form, that human beings might copy it; and behold, it was full of grace and truth.

The Life of grace and truth; that is the Life of Christ, and, therefore, the Life of God.

The Life of grace—of graciousness, love, pity, generosity, usefulness, self-sacrifice; the Life of truth —of faithfulness, fairness, justice, the desire to impart knowledge, and to guide men into all truth. The Life, in one word, of charity, which is both grace and truth, both love and justice, in one Eternal essence. That is the life which God lives for ever in heaven. That is The one Eternal Life, which must be also the Life of God. For, as there is but one Eternal, even God, so is there but one Eternal Life, which is the life of God and of His Christ. And the Spirit by which it is inspired into the hearts of men is the Spirit of God, who proceedeth alike from the Father and from the Son.

Have you not seen men and women in whom these words have been literally and palpably fulfilled? Have you not seen those who, though old in years, were so young in heart, that they seem to have drunk of the Fountain of perpetual Youth,—in whom, though the outward body decayed, the soul was renewed day by day; who kept fresh and pure the noblest and holiest instincts of their childhood, and went on adding to them the experience, the calm, the charity of age? Persons whose eye was still so bright, whose smile was still so tender, that it seemed that they could never die? And when they died, or seemed to die, you felt that THEY were not dead, but only their husk and shell; that they themselves, the character which you had loved and reverenced, must endure on, beyond the grave, beyond the worlds, in a literally Everlasting Life, independent of nature, and of all the changes of the material universe.

Surely you have seen such. And surely what you loved in them was the Spirit of God Himself,—that love, joy, peace, longsuffering, gentleness, goodness, which the natural savage man has not. Has not, I say, look at him where you will, from the tropics to the pole, because it is a gift above man; the gift of the Spirit of God; the Eternal Life of goodness, which natural birth cannot give to man, nor natural death take away.

You have surely seen such persons—if you have not, *I* have, thank God, full many a time;—but if you have seen them, did you not see this?—That it was not riches which gave them this Life, if they were rich; or intellect, if they were clever; or science, if they were learned; or rank, if they were cultivated; or bodily organization, if they were beautiful and strong: that this noble and gentle life of theirs was independent of their body, of their mind, of their circumstances? Nay, have you not seen this,—*I* have, thank God, full many a time,—'That not many rich, not many mighty, not many noble are called: but that God's strength is rather made perfect in man's weakness,—that in foul garrets, in lonely sick-beds, in dark places of the earth, you find ignorant people, sickly people, ugly people, stupid people, in spite of, in defiance of, every opposing circumstance, leading heroic lives,—a blessing, a comfort, an example, a very Fount of Life to all around them; and dying heroic deaths, because they know they have Eternal Life?

And what was that which had made them different from the mean, the savage, the drunken, the profligate beings around them? This at least. That they were of those of whom it is written, 'Let him that is athirst come.' They had been athirst for Life. They had had instincts and longings; very simple and humble, but very pure and noble. At times, it may be, they had been unfaithful to those instincts. At times, it may be, they had fallen. They had said: 'Why should I not do like the rest, and be a savage? Let me eat and drink, for to-morrow I die;' and they had cast themselves down into sin, for very weariness and heaviness, and were for a while as the beasts which have no law.

But the thirst after The noble Life was too deep to be quenched in that foul puddle. It endured, and it conquered; and they became more and more true to it, till it was satisfied at last, though never quenched, that thirst of theirs, in Him who alone can satisfy it—the God who gave it; for in them were fulfilled the Lord's own words: 'Blessed are they that hunger and thirst after righteousness, for they shall be filled.'

There are those, I fear, in this church—there are too many in all churches—who have not felt, as yet, this divine thirst after a higher Life; who wish not for an Eternal, but for a merely endless life, and who would not care greatly what sort of life that endless life might be, if only it was not too unlike the life which they live now; who would be glad enough to continue as they are, in their selfish pleasure, selfish gain, selfish content, for ever; who look on death as an unpleasant necessity, the end of all which they really prize; and who have taken up religion chiefly as a means for escaping still more unpleasant necessities after death. To them, as to all, it is said, 'Come, and drink of the water of life freely.' But The Life of goodness which Christ offers, is not the life they want. Wherefore they will not come to Him, that they may have life. Meanwhile, they have no right to sneer at the Fountain of Youth, or the Cup of Immortality. Well were it for them if those dreams were true; in their heart of hearts they know it. Would they not go to the ends of the earth to bathe in the Fountain of Youth? Would they not give all their gold for a draught of the Cup of Immortality, and so save themselves, once and for all, the trouble of becoming good?

But there are those here, I doubt not, who have in them, by grace of God, that same divine thirst for the Higher Life; who are discontented with themselves, ashamed of themselves; who are tormented by longings which they cannot satisfy, instincts which they cannot analyse, powers which they cannot employ, duties which they cannot perform, doctrinal confusions which they cannot unravel; who would welcome any change, even the most tremendous, which would make them nobler, purer, juster, more loving, more useful, more clear-headed and sound-minded; and when they think of death say with the poet,—

> "'Tis life, not death for which I pant,
> 'Tis life, whereof my nerves are scant,
> More life, and fuller, that I want.'

To them I say—for God has said it long ago,—Be of good cheer. The calling and gifts of God are without repentance. If you have the divine thirst, it will be surely satisfied. If you long to be better men and women, better men and women you will surely be. Only be true to those higher instincts; only do not learn to despise and quench that divine thirst; only struggle on, in spite of mistakes, of failures, even of sins —for every one of which last your heavenly Father will chastise you, even while He forgives; in spite of all falls, struggle on. Blessed are you that hunger and thirst after righteousness, for you shall be filled. To you— and not in vain—'The Spirit and the Bride say, Come. And let him that heareth say, Come. And let him that is athirst come. And whosoever will, let him drink of the water of life freely.'

SERMON II.

THE PHYSICIAN'S CALLING.

(Preached at Whitehall for St. George's Hospital)

ST. MATTHEW ix. 35.

And Jesus went about all the cities and villages, teaching in their synagogues, and preaching the gospel of the kingdom, and healing every sickness and every disease among the people.

THE Gospels speak of disease and death in a very simple and human tone. They regard them in theory, as all are forced to regard them in fact, as sore and sad evils.

The Gospels never speak of disease or death as necessities; never as the will of God. It is Satan, not God, who binds the woman with a spirit of infirmity. It is not the will of our Father in heaven that one little one should perish. Indeed, we do not sufficiently appreciate the abhorrence with which the whole of Scripture speaks of disease and death: because we are in the habit of interpreting many texts which speak of the disease and death of the body in this life as if they referred to the punishment and death of the soul in the world to come. We have a perfect right to do that; for Scripture tells us that there is a mysterious analogy and likeness between the life of the body and that of the soul, and therefore between the death of the body and that of the soul: but we must not forget, in the secondary and higher spiritual interpretation of such texts, their primary and physical meaning, which is this —that disease and death are uniformly throughout Scripture held up to the abhorrence of man.

Moreover—and this is noteworthy—the Gospels, and indeed all Scripture, very seldom palliate the misery of disease, by drawing from it those moral lessons which we ourselves do. I say very seldom. The Bible does so here and there, to tell us that we may do so likewise. And we may thank God heartily that the Bible does so. It would be a miserable world, if all that the clergyman or the friend might say by the sick-bed were, 'This is an inevitable evil, like hail and thunder. You must bear it if you can: and if not, then not.' A miserable world, if he could not say with full belief, '" My son, despise not thou the chastening of the Lord, nor faint when thou art rebuked of Him. For whom the Lord loveth He chasteneth, and scourgeth every son whom He receiveth." Thou knowest not now why thou art afflicted; perhaps thou wilt never know in this life. But a day will come when thou wilt know: when thou wilt find that this sickness came to thee at the exact right time, in the exact right way; when thou wilt find that God has been keeping thee in the secret place of His presence from the provoking of men, and hiding thee privately in His tabernacle from the spite of tongues; when thou wilt discover that thou hast been learning precious lessons for thy immortal spirit, while thou didst seem to thyself merely tossing with clouded intellect on a bed of useless pain; when thou wilt find that God was nearest to thee, at the very moment when He seemed to have left thee most utterly.'

Thank God, we can say that, and more; and we will say it. But we must bear in mind, that the Gospels, which are the very parts of Scripture which speak most concerning disease, omit almost entirely that cheering and comforting view of it.

And why? Only to force upon our attention, I believe a view even more cheering and comforting: a view deeper and wider, because supplied not merely to the pious sufferer, but to all sufferers; not merely to the Christian, but to all mankind. And that is, I believe, none other than this: that God does not only bring spiritual good out of physical evil, but that He hates physical evil itself: that He desires not only the salvation of our souls, but the health of our bodies, and that when He sent His only begotten Son into the world to do His will, part of that will was, that He should attack and conquer the physical evil of disease—

as it were instinctively, as his natural enemy, and directly, for the sake of the body of the sufferer.

Many excellent men, seeing how the healing of disease was an integral part of our Lord's mission, and of the mission of His apostles, have wished that it should likewise form an integral part of the mission of the Church: that the clergy should as much as possible be physicians; the physician, as much as possible, a clergyman. The plan may be useful in exceptional cases—in that, for instance, of the missionary among the heathen.

But experience has decided, that in a civilized and Christian country it had better be otherwise: that the great principle of the division of labour should be carried out: that there should be in the land a body of men whose whole mind and time should be devoted to one part only of our Lord's work—the battle with disease and death. And the effect has been not to lower but to raise the medical profession. It has saved the doctor from one great danger—that of abusing, for the purposes of religious proselytizing, the unlimited confidence reposed in him. It has freed him from many a superstition which enfeebled and confused the physicians of the Middle Ages. It has enabled him to devote his whole intellect to physical science, till he has set his art on a sound and truly scientific foundation. It has enabled him to attack physical evil with a single-hearted energy and devotion which ought to command the respect and admiration of his fellow-countrymen. If all classes did their work half as simply, as bravely, as determinedly, as unselfishly, as the medical men of Great Britain—and, I doubt not, of other countries in Europe—this world would be a far fairer place than it is likely to be for many a year to come. It is good to do one thing and to do it well. It is good to follow Christ in one thing, and to follow Him utterly in that. And the medical man has set his mind to do one thing,—to hate calmly, but with an internecine hatred, disease and death, and to fight against them to the end.

The medical man is complained of at times as being too materialistic—as caring more for the bodies of his patients than for their souls. Do not blame him too hastily. In his exclusive care for the body, he may be witnessing unconsciously, yet mightily, for the soul, for God, for the Bible, for immortality.

Is he not witnessing for God, when he shows by his acts that he believes God to be a God of Life, not of death; of health, not of disease; of order, not of disorder; of joy and strength, not of misery and weakness?

Is he not witnessing for Christ when, like Christ, he heals all manner of sickness and disease among the people, and attacks physical evil as the natural foe of man and of the Creator of man?

Is he not witnessing for the immortality of the soul when he fights against death as an evil to be postponed at all hazards and by all means, even when its advent is certain? Surely it is so. How often have we seen the doctor by the dying bed, trying to preserve life, when he knew well that life could not be preserved! We have been tempted to say to him, 'Let the sufferer alone. He is senseless. He is going. We can do nothing more for his soul; you can do nothing more for his body. Why torment him needlessly for the sake of a few more moments of respiration? Let him alone to die in peace.' How have we been tempted to say that? We have not dared to say it; for we saw that the doctor, and not we, was in the right; that in all those little efforts, so wise, so anxious, so tender, so truly chivalrous, to keep the failing breath for a few moments more in the body of one who had no earthly claim upon his care, that doctor was bearing a testimony, unconscious yet most weighty, to that human instinct of which the Bible approves throughout, that death in a human being is an evil, an anomaly, a curse; against which, though he could not rescue the man from the clutch of his foe, he was bound, in duty and honour, to fight until the last, simply because it was death, and death was the enemy of man.

But if the medical man bears witness for God and spiritual things when he seems exclusively occupied with the body, so does the hospital. Look at those noble buildings which the generosity of our fellow-countrymen have erected in all our great cities. You may find in them, truly, sermons in stones; sermons for rich alike and poor. They preach to the rich, these hospitals, that the sick-bed levels all alike; that they are the equals and brothers of the poor in the terrible liability to suffer! They preach to the poor that they are, through Christianity, the equals of the rich in their means and opportunities of cure. I say through Christianity. Whether the founders so intended or not (and those who founded most of them, St. George's among the rest, did so intend), these hospitals bear direct witness for Christ. They do this, and would do it, even if—which God forbid—the name of Christ were never mentioned within their walls. That may seem a paradox; but it is none. For it is a historic fact, that hospitals are a creation of Christian times, and of Christian men. The heathen knew them not. In that great city of ancient Rome, as far as I have ever been able to discover, there was not a single hospital,—not even, I fear, a single charitable institution. Fearful thought—a city of a million and a half inhabitants, the centre of human civilization: and not a hospital there! The Roman Dives paid his physician; the Roman Lazarus literally lay at his gate full of sores, till he died the death of the street dogs which licked those sores, and was carried forth to be thrust under ground awhile, till the same dogs came to quarrel over his bones. The misery and helplessness of the lower classes in the great cities of the Roman empire, till the Church of Christ arose, literally with healing in its wings, cannot, I believe, be exaggerated.

Eastern piety, meanwhile, especially among the Hindoos, had founded hospitals, in the old meaning of that word—namely, almshouses for the infirm and aged: but I believe there is no record of hospitals, like our modern ones, for the cure of disease, till Christianity spread over the Western world.

And why? Because then first men began to feel the mighty truth contained in the text. If Christ were a healer, His servants must be healers likewise. If Christ regarded physical evil as a direct evil, so must they. If Christ fought against it with all His power, so must they, with such power as He revealed to them. And so arose exclusively in the Christian mind, a feeling not only of the nobleness of the healing art, but of the religious duty of exercising that art on every human being who needed it; and hospitals are to be counted, as a historic fact, among the many triumphs of the Gospel.

If there be any one—especially a working man—in this church this day who is inclined to undervalue the Bible and Christianity, let him know that, but for the Bible and Christianity, he has not the slightest reason to believe that there would have been at this moment a hospital in London to receive him and his in the hour of sickness or disabling accident, and to lavish on him there, unpaid as the light and air of God outside, every resource of science, care, generosity, and tenderness, simply because he is a human being. Yes; truly catholic are these hospitals,—catholic as the bounty of our heavenly Father,—without respect of persons, giving to all liberally and upbraiding not, like Him in whom all live, and move, and have their being; witnesses better than all our sermons for the universal bounty and tolerance of that heavenly Father who causes the sun to shine on the evil and the good, and his rain to fall upon the just and on the unjust, and is perfect in this, that He is good to the unthankful and the evil.

And, therefore, the preacher can urge his countrymen, let their opinions, creed, tastes, be what they may, to support hospitals with especial freedom, earnestness, and confidence. Heaven forbid that I should undervalue any charitable institution whatever. May God's blessing be on them all. But this I have a right to say, —that whatever objections, suspicions, prejudices there may be concerning any other form of charity, concerning hospitals there can be none. Every farthing bestowed on them must go toward the direct doing of good. There is no fear in them of waste, of misapplication of funds, of private jobbery, of ulterior and unavowed objects. Palpable and unmistakeable good is all they do and all they can do. And he who gives to a hospital has the comfort of knowing that he is bestowing a direct blessing on the bodies of his fellow-men; and it may be on their souls likewise.

For I have said that these hospitals witness silently for God and for Christ; and I must believe that that silent witness is not lost on the minds of thousands who enter them. It sinks in,—all the more readily because it is not thrust upon them,—and softens and breaks up their hearts to receive the precious seed of the word of God. Many a man, too ready from bitter experience to believe that his fellow-men cared not for him, has entered the wards of a hospital to be happily undeceived. He finds that he is cared for; that he is not forgotten either by God or man; that there is a place for him, too, at God's table, in his hour of utmost need; and angels of God, in human form, ready to minister to his necessities; and, softened by that discovery, he has listened humbly, perhaps for the first time in his life, to the exhortations of a clergyman; and has taken in, in the hour of dependence and weakness, the lessons which he was too proud or too sullen to hear in the day of independence and sturdy health. And so do these hospitals, it seems to me, follow the example and practice of our Lord Himself, who, by ministering to the animal wants and animal sufferings of the people, by showing them that He sympathised with those lower sorrows of which they were most immediately conscious, made them follow Him gladly, and listen to Him with faith, when He proclaimed to them in words of wisdom, that Father in heaven whom He had already proclaimed to them in acts of mercy.

And now, I have to appeal to you for the excellent and honourable foundation of St. George's Hospital. I might speak to you, and speak, too, with a personal reverence and affection of many years' standing, of the claims of that noble institution; of the illustrious men of science who have taught within its walls; of the number of able and honourable young men who go forth out of it, year by year, to carry their blessed and truly divine art, not only over Great Britain, but to the islands of the farthest seas. But to say that would be merely to say what is true, thank God, of every hospital in London.

One fact only, therefore, I shall urge, which gives St. George's Hospital special claims on the attention of the rich.

Situated, as it is, in the very centre of the west end of London, it is the special refuge of those who are most especially of service to the dwellers in the West-end. Those who are used up—fairly or unfairly—in ministering to the luxuries of the high-born and wealthy:

the groom thrown in the park; the housemaid crippled by lofty stairs; the workman fallen from the scaffolding of the great man's palace; the footman or coachman who has contracted disease from long hours of nightly exposure, while his master and mistress have been warm and gay at rout and ball; and those, too, whose number, I fear, are very great, who contract disease, themselves, their wives, and children, from actual want, when they are thrown suddenly out of employ at the end of the season, and London is said to be empty—of all but two million of living souls :—the great majority of these crowd into St. George's Hospital to find there relief and comfort, which those to whom they minister are solemnly bound to supply by their contributions. The rich and well-born of this land are very generous. They are doing their duty, on the whole, nobly and well. Let them do their duty—the duty which literally lies nearest them—by St. George's Hospital, and they will wipe off a stain, not on the hospital, but on the rich people in its neighbourhood—the stain of that hospital's debts.

The deficiency in the funds of the hospital for the year 1862-3—caused, be it remembered, by no extravagance or sudden change, but simply by the necessity for succouring those who would otherwise have been destitute of succour—the deficiency, I say, on an expenditure of 15,000*l.* amounts to more than 3,200*l.* which has had to be met by selling out funded property, and so diminishing the capital of the institution. Ought this to be? I ask. Ought this to be, while more wealth is collected within half a mile of that hospital than in any spot of like extent in the globe?

My friends, this is the time of Lent; the time whereof it is written,—'Is not this the fast which I have chosen, to deal thy bread to the hungry, and bring the poor that is cast out to thine house? when thou seest the naked that thou cover him, and that thou hide not thyself from thine own flesh? If thou let thy soul go forth to the hungry, and satisfy the afflicted soul, then shall thy light rise in obscurity, and thy darkness be as the noonday. And the Lord shall guide thee continually, and satisfy thy soul, and make fat thy bones, and thou shalt be like a watered garden, and as a spring that doth not fail.'

Let us obey that command literally, and see whether the promise is not literally fulfilled to us in return.

SERMON III.

THE VICTORY OF LIFE.

(Preached at the Chapel Royal.)

ISAIAH xxxviii. 18, 19.

The grave cannot praise thee, death cannot celebrate thee: they that go down into the pit cannot hope for thy truth. The living, the living, he shall praise thee.

I MAY seem to have taken a strange text on which to speak,—a mournful, a seemingly hopeless text. Why I have chosen it, I trust that you will see presently; certainly not that I may make you hopeless about death. Meanwhile, let us consider it; for it is in the Bible, and, like all words in the Bible, was written for our instruction.

Now it is plain, I think, that the man who said these words—good king Hezekiah—knew nothing of what we call heaven; of a blessed life with God after death. He looks on death as his end. If he dies, he says, he will not see the Lord in the land of the living, any more than he will see man with the inhabitants of the world. God's mercies, he thinks, will end with his death. God can only show His mercy and truth by saving him from death. For the grave cannot praise God, death cannot celebrate Him; those who go down into the pit cannot hope for His truth. The living, the living, shall praise God; as Hezekiah praises Him that day, because God has cured him of his sickness, and added fifteen years to his life.

No language can be plainer than this. A man who had believed that he would go to heaven when he died could not have used it.

In many of the Psalms, likewise, you will find words of exactly the same kind, which show that the men who wrote them had no clear conception, if any conception at all, of a life after death.

Solomon's words about death are utterly awful from their sadness. With him, 'that which befalleth the sons of men befalleth beasts; as one dieth, so dieth the other. Yea, they have all one breath, so that a man hath no pre-eminence over a beast, and all is vanity. All go to one place, all are of the dust, and all turn to dust again. Who knoweth the spirit of man that goeth upward, and the spirit of the beast that goeth downward to the earth?'

He knows nothing about it. All he knows is, that the spirit shall return to God who gave it,—and that a man will surely find, in this life, a recompence for all his deeds, whether good or evil.

'Remember therefore thy Creator in the days of thy youth, while the evil days come not, nor the years draw nigh, when thou shalt say, I have no pleasure in them.... Fear God, and keep His commandments; for this is the whole duty of man. For God shall bring every work into judgment, with every secret thing, whether it be good, or whether it be evil.'

This is the doctrine of the Old Testament; that God judges and rewards and punishes men in this life: but as for death, it is a great black cloud into which all men must enter, and see and be seen no more. Only twice or thrice, perhaps, a gleam of light from beyond breaks through the dark. David, the noblest and wisest of all the Jews, can say once that God will not leave his soul in hell, neither suffer His holy one to see corruption; Job says that, though after his skin worms destroy his body, yet in his flesh he shall see God; and Isaiah, again, when he sees his countrymen slaughtered, and his nation all but destroyed, can say, 'Thy dead men shall live, together with my dead body shall they arise. Awake and sing, ye that dwell in dust: for thy dew is as the dew of the morning, which brings the parched herbs to life and freshness again.'— Great and glorious sayings, all of them: but we cannot tell how far either David, or Job, or Isaiah, were thinking of a life after death. We can think of a life after death when we use them; for we know how they have been fulfilled in Jesus Christ our Lord; and we can see in them more than the Jews of old could do; for, like all inspired words, they mean more than the men who wrote them thought of; but we have no right to impute our Christianity to them.

The only undoubted picture, perhaps, of the next life to be found in the Old Testament, is that grand one in Isaiah xiv., where he paints to us the tyrant king of Babylon going down into hell :—

'Hell from beneath is moved for thee, to meet thee at thy coming; it stirreth up the dead for thee, even all the chief ones of the earth; it hath raised up from their thrones all the kings of the nations. All they shall speak and say unto thee, Art thou also become weak as we? art thou become like unto us? Thy pomp is brought down to the grave, and the noise of thy viols: the worm is spread under thee, and the worms cover thee. How art thou fallen from heaven, O Lucifer, son of the morning! how art thou cut down to the ground, which didst weaken the nations!'——Awful and grand enough: but quite different, you will observe, from the notions of hell which are common now-a-days; and much more like those which we read in the old Greek poets, and especially, in the Necyomanteia of the Odyssey.

When it was that the Jews gained any fuller notions about the next life, it is very difficult to say. Certainly not before they were carried away captive to Babylon. After that they began to mix much with the great nations of the East: with Greeks, Persians, and Indians; and from them, most probably, they learned to believe in a heaven after death to which good men would go, and a fiery hell to which bad men would go. At least, the heathen nations round them, and our forefathers likewise, believed in some sort of heaven and hell, hundreds of years before the coming of our blessed Lord.

The Jews had learned, also—at least the Pharisees— to believe in the resurrection of the dead. Martha speaks of it; and St. Paul, when he tells the Pharisees that, having been brought up a Pharisee, he was on their side against the Sadducees.—'I am a Pharisee, he says, 'the son of a Pharisee; for the hope of the resurrection of the dead I am called in question.'

But if it be so,—if St. Paul and the Apostles believed in heaven and hell, and the resurrection of the dead, before they became Christians, what more did they learn about the next life, when they became Christians? Something they did learn, most certainly—and that most important. St. Paul speaks of what our Lord and our Lord's resurrection had taught him, as something quite infinitely grander, and more blessed, than what he had known before. He talks of our Lord as having abolished death, and brought life and immortality to light;

of His having conquered death, and of His destroying death at last. He speaks at moments as if he did not expect to die at all; and when he does speak of the death of the Christian, it is merely as a falling asleep. When he speaks of his own death, it is merely as a change of place. He longs to depart, and to be with Christ. Death had looked terrible to him once, when he was a Jew. Death had had a sting, and the grave a victory, which seemed ready to conquer him: but now he cries, 'O Death, where is thy sting? O Grave, where is thy victory?' and then he declares that the terrors of death and the grave are taken away, not by anything which he knew when he was a Pharisee, but through our Lord Jesus Christ.

All his old Jewish notions of the resurrection, though they were true as far as they went, seemed poor and paltry beside what Christ had taught him. He was not going to wait till the end of the world—perhaps for thousands of years—in darkness and the shadow of death, he knew not where or how. His soul was to pass at once into life,—into joy, and peace, and bliss, in the presence of his Saviour, till it should have a new body given to it, in the resurrection of life at the last day.

This, I think, is what St. Paul learned, and what the Jews had not learned till our blessed Lord came. They were still afraid of death. It looked to them a dark and ugly blank; and no wonder. For would it not be dark and ugly enough to have to wait, we know not where, it may be a thousand, it may be tens of thousands of years, till the resurrection in the last day, before we entered into joy, peace, activity or anything worthy of the name of life? Would not death have a sting indeed, the grave a victory indeed, if we had to be as good as dead for ten thousands of years?

What then? Remember this, that death is an enemy, an evil thing, an enemy to man, and therefore an enemy to Christ, the King and Head and Saviour of man. Men ought not to die, and they feel it. It is no use to tell them, 'Everything that is born must die, and why not you? All other animals died. They died, just as they die now, hundreds of thousands of years before man came upon this earth; and why should man expect to have a different lot? Why should you not take your death patiently, as you take any other evil which you cannot escape?' The heart of man, as soon as he begins to be a man, and not a mere savage; as soon as he begins to think reasonably, and feel deeply; the heart of man answers: 'No, I am not a mere animal. I have something in me which ought not to die, which perhaps cannot die. I have a living soul in me, which ought to be able to keep my body alive likewise, but cannot; and therefore death is my enemy. I hate him, and I believe that I was meant to hate him. Something must be wrong with me, or I should not die; something must be wrong with all mankind, or I should not see those I love dying round me.'

Yes, my friends, death is an enemy,—a hideous, hateful thing. The longer one looks at it, the more one hates it. The more often one sees it, the less one grows accustomed to it. Its very commonness makes it all the more shocking. We may not be so much shocked at seeing the old die. We say, 'They have done their work, why should they not go?' That is not true. They have not done their work. There is more work in plenty for them to do, if they could but live; and it seems shocking and sad, at least to him who loves his country and his kind, that, just as men have grown old enough to be of use, when they have learnt to conquer their passions, when their characters are formed, when they have gained sound experience of this world, and what man ought and can do in it,—just as, in fact, they have become most able to teach and help their fellow-men,—that then they are to grow old, and decrepit, and helpless, and fade away, and die just when they are most fit to live, and the world needs them most.

Sad, I say, and strange is that. But sadder, and more strange, and more utterly shocking, to see the young die; to see parents leaving infant children,

children vanishing early out of the world where they might have done good work for God and man.

What arguments will make us believe that that ought to be? That that is God's will? That that is anything but an evil, an anomaly, a disease?

Not the Bible, certainly. The Bible never tells us that such tragedies as are too often seen are the will of God. The Bible says that it is not the will of our Father that one of these little ones should perish. The Bible tells us that Jesus, when on earth, went about fighting and conquering disease and death, even raising from the dead those who had died before their time. To fight against death, and to give life wheresoever He went—that was His work; by that He proclaimed the will of God, His Father, that none should perish, who sent His Son that men might have life, and have it more abundantly. By that He declared that death was an evil and a disorder among men, which He would some day crush and destroy utterly, that mortality should be swallowed up of life.

And yet we die, and shall die. Yes. The body is dead, because of sin. Mankind is a diseased race; and it must pay the penalty of its sins for many an age to come, and die, and suffer, and sorrow. But not for ever. For what mean such words as these—for something they must mean?—

'If a man keep my saying, he shall never see death.'

And again, 'He that believeth in Me, though he were dead, yet shall he live; and he that liveth and believeth in Me shall never die.'

Do such words as these mean only that we shall rise again in the resurrection at the last day? Surely not. Our Lord spoke them in answer to that very notion.

'Martha said to Him, I know that my brother shall rise again, in the resurrection at the last day. Jesus said unto her, I *am* the resurrection and the life;' and then showed what He meant by bringing back Lazarus to life, unchanged, and as he had been before he died.

Surely, if that miracle meant anything, if these words meant anything, it meant this: that those who die in the fear of God, and in the faith of Christ, do not really taste death; that to them there is no death, but only a change of place, a change of state; that they pass at once, and instantly, into some new life, with all their powers, all their feelings, unchanged,—purified doubtless from earthly stains, but still the same living, thinking, active beings which they were here on earth. I say, active. The Bible says nothing about their sleeping till the Day of Judgment, as some have fancied. Rest they may; rest they will, if they need rest. But what is the true rest? Not idleness, but peace of mind. To rest from sin, from sorrow, from fear, from doubt, from care,—this is the true rest. Above all, to rest from the worst weariness of all—knowing one's duty, and yet not being able to do it. That is true rest; the rest of God, who works for ever, and yet is at rest for ever; as the stars over our heads move for ever, thousands of miles each day, and yet are at perfect rest, because they move orderly, harmoniously, fulfilling the law which God has given them. Perfect rest, in perfect work; that surely is the rest of blessed spirits, till the final consummation of all things, when Christ shall have made up the number of His elect.

I hope that this is so. I trust that this is so. I think our Lord's great words can mean nothing less than this. And if it be so, what comfort for us who must die? What comfort for us who have seen others die, if death be but a new birth into some higher life; if all that it changes in us is our body—the mere shell and husk of us—such a change as comes over the snake, when he casts his old skin, and comes out fresh and gay, or even the crawling caterpillar, which breaks its prison, and spreads its wings to the sun as a fair butterfly. Where is the sting of death, then, if death can sting, and poison, and corrupt nothing of us for which our friends have loved us; nothing of us with which we could do service to men or God? Where is the victory of the grave, if, so far from the grave holding us down, it frees us from the very thing which holds us down,—the mortal body?

Death is not death, then, if it kills no part of us, save that which hindered us from perfect life. Death is not death, if it raises us in a moment from darkness into light, from weakness into strength, from sinfulness into holiness. Death is not death, if it brings us nearer to Christ, who is the fount of life. Death is not death, if it perfects our faith by sight, and lets us behold Him in whom we have believed. Death is not death, if it gives us to those whom we have loved and lost, for whom we have lived, for whom we long to live again. Death is not death, if it joins the child to the mother who is gone before. Death is not death, if it takes away from that mother for ever all a mother's anxieties, a mother's fears, and lets her see, in the gracious countenance of her Saviour, a sure and certain pledge that those whom she has left behind are safe, safe with Christ and in Christ, through all the chances and dangers of his mortal life. Death is not death, if it rids us of doubt and fear, of chance and change, of space and time, and all which space and time bring forth, and then destroy. Death is not death; for Christ has conquered death, for Himself, and for those who trust in Him. And to those who say, 'You were born in time, and in time you must die, as all other creatures do; Time is your king and lord, as he has been of all the old worlds before this, and of all the races of beasts, whose bones and shells lie fossil in the rocks of a thousand generations;' then we can answer them, in the words of the wise man, and in the name of Christ who conquered death :—

> 'Fly, envious time, till thou run out thy race,
> And glut thyself with what thy womb devours,
> Which is no more than what is false and vain
> And merely mortal dross.
> So little is our loss, so little is thy gain.
> For when as each bad thing thou hast entombed,
> And, last of all, thy greedy self consumed,
> Then long eternity shall greet our bliss
> With an individual kiss,
> And joy shall overtake us as a flood,
> When everything that is sincerely good
> And perfectly divine,
> And truth, and peace, and love shall ever shine
> About the supreme throne
> Of Him, unto whose happy-making sight alone
> When once our heavenly-guided soul shall climb,
> Then all this earthly grossness quit,
> Attired with stars, we shall for ever sit
> Triumphant over death, and chance, and thee, O Time!'

SERMON IV.
THE WAGES OF SIN.
(Chapel Royal, June, 1864.)

ROM. vi. 21—23.

What fruit had ye then in those things whereof ye are now ashamed? for the end of those things is death. But now being made free from sin, and become servants to God, ye have your fruit unto holiness, and the end everlasting life. For the wages of sin is death; but the gift of God is eternal life through Jesus Christ our Lord.

THIS is a glorious text, if we will only believe it simply, and take it as it stands.

But if in place of St. Paul's words we put quite different words of our own, and say—By 'the wages of sin is death,' St. Paul means that the punishment of sin is eternal life in torture, then we say something which may be true, but which is not what St. Paul is speaking of here. For wages are not punishment, and death is not eternal life in torture, any more than in happiness.

That, one would think, was clear. It is our duty to take St. Paul's words, if we really believe them to be inspired, simply as they stand; and if we do not quite understand them, to explain them by St. Paul's own words about these matters in other parts of his writings.

St. Paul was an inspired Apostle. Let him speak for himself. Surely he knew best what he wished to say, and how to say it.

Now St. Paul's opinions about death and eternal life are very clear; for he speaks of them often, and at great length.

He considered that the great enemy of God and man, the last enemy Christ would destroy, was death; and that, after death was destroyed, the end would come, when God would be all in all. Then came the question, which has puzzled men in all ages—How death came into the world. St. Paul answers, By sin. He says, as the author of the third chapter of Genesis says, that Adam became subject to death by his fall. By one man, he says, sin entered into the world, and death by sin, and so death passed upon all men, for that all have sinned. And thus, he says, death reigned even over those who had not sinned after the likeness of Adam's transgression.

That he is speaking of bodily death is clear, because he is always putting it in contrast to the resurrection to life,—not merely to a spiritual resurrection from the death of sin to the life of righteousness; but to the resurrection of the body,—to our Lord's being raised from the dead, that He might die no more.

Then he speaks of eternal life. He always speaks of it as an actual life, in a spiritual body, into which our mortal bodies are to be changed. Nothing can be clearer from what he says in 1 Cor. xv., that he means an actual rising again of our bodies from bodily death; an actual change in them; an actual life in them for ever.

But he says, again and again,—As sin caused the death of the body, so righteousness is to cause its life.

'When ye were the servants of sin,' he says to the Romans, 'what fruit had ye in those things whereof ye are now ashamed? For the end of those things is death. But now being made free from sin, and become servants to God, ye have your fruit unto holiness, and the end everlasting life. For the wages of sin is death; but the gift of God is eternal life through Jesus Christ our Lord.'

This is St. Paul's opinion. And we shall do well to believe it, and to learn from it, this day, and all days.

The wages of sin and the end of sin is death. Not the punishment of sin; but something much worse. The wages of sin, and the end of sin.

And how is that worse news? My friends, every sinner knows so well in his heart that it is worse news, more terrible news, for him, that he tries to persuade himself that death is only the arbitrary punishment of his sin; or, quite as often, that the punishment of his sin is not even death, but eternal torment in the next life.

And why? Because, as long as he can believe that death, or hell, are only punishments arbitrarily fixed by God against his sins, he can hope that God will let him off the punishment. Die, he knows he must, because all men die; and so he makes up his mind to that: but being sent to hell after he dies, is so very terrible a punishment, that he cannot believe that God will be so hard on him as that. No; he will get off, and be forgiven at last somehow, for surely God will not condemn him to hell. And so he finds it very convenient and comfortable to believe in hell, just because he does not believe that he is going there, whoever else may be.

But, it is a very terrible, heartrending thought, for a man to find out that what he will receive is not punishment, but wages; not punishment but the end of the very road which he is travelling on. That the wages of sin, and the end of sin, to which it must lead, are death; that every time he sins he is earning those wages, deserving them, meriting them, and therefore receiving them by the just laws of the world of God. That does torment him, that does terrify him, if he will look steadfastly at the broad plain fact—You need not dream of being let off, respited, reprieved, pardoned in any way. The thing cannot be done. It is contrary to the laws of God and of God's universe. It is as impossible as that fire should not burn, or water run up hill. It is not a question of arbitrary punishment, which may be arbitrarily remitted; but of wages, which you needs must take, weekly, daily, and hourly; and those wages are death: a question of travelling on a certain road, whereon, if you travel it long enough, you must come to the end of it; and the end is death. Your sins are killing you by inches; all day long they are sowing in you the seeds of disease and death. Every sin which you commit with your body shortens your bodily life. Every sin you commit with your mind, every act of stupidity, folly, wilful ignorance, helps to destroy your mind, and leave you dull, silly, devoid of right reason. Every sin you commit with your spirit, each sin of passion and temper, envy and malice, pride and vanity, injustice and cruelty, extravagance and self-indulgence, helps to destroy your spiritual life, and leave you bad, more and more unable to do the right and avoid the wrong, more and more unable to discern right from wrong; and that last is spiritual death, the eternal death of your moral being. There are three parts in you—body, mind, and spirit; and every sin you commit helps to kill one of these three, and, in many cases, to kill all three together.

So, sinner, dream not of escaping punishment at the last. You are being punished now, for you are punishing yourself; and you will continue to be punished for ever, for you will be punishing yourself for ever, as long as you go on doing wrong, and breaking the laws which God has appointed for body, mind and spirit. You can see that a drunkard is killing himself, body and mind, by drink. You see that he knows that, poor wretch, as well as you. He knows that every time he gets drunk he is cutting so much off his life; and yet he cannot help it. He knows that drink is poison, and yet he goes back to his poison.

Then know, habitual sinner, that you are like that drunkard. That every bad habit in which you indulge is shortening the life of some of your faculties, and that God Himself cannot save you from the doom which you are earning, deserving, and working out for yourself every day and every hour.

Oh how men hate that message!—the message that the true wrath of God, necessary, inevitable, is revealed from heaven against all unrighteousness of men. How they writhe under it! How they shut their ears to it, and cry to their preachers, 'No! Tell us of any wrath of God but that! Tell us rather of the torments of the damned, of a frowning God, of absolute decrees to destruction, of the reprobation of millions before they are born; any doctrine, however fearful and horrible: because we don't quite believe it, but only think that we ought to believe it. Yes, tell us anything rather than that news, which cuts at the root of all our pride, of all our comfort, and all our superstition—the news that we cannot escape the consequences of our own actions; that there are no back stairs up which we may be smuggled into heaven; that as we sow, so we shall reap; that we are filled with the fruits of our own devices; every man his own poisoner, every man his own executioner, every man his own suicide; that hell begins in this life, and death begins before we die :—do not say that: because we cannot help believing it; for our own consciousness and our own experience tell us it is true.' No wonder that the preacher who tells men that is hated, is called a Rationalist, a Pantheist, a heretic, and what not, just because he does set forth such a living God, such a justice of God, such a wrath of God as would make the sinner tremble, if he believed in it, not merely once in a way, when he hears a stirring sermon about the endless torments: but all day long, going out and coming in, lying on his bed and walking by the way, always haunted by the shadow of himself, knowing that he is bearing about in him the perpetually growing death of sin.

And still more painful would this message be to the

sinner, if he had any kindly feeling for others; and, thank God, there are few who have not that. For St. Paul's message to him is, that the wages of his sin is death, not merely to himself, but to others—to his family and children above all. So St. Paul declares in what he says of his doctrine of original or birth sin, by which, as the Article says, every man is very far gone from original righteousness, and is of his own nature inclined to evil, so that the flesh lusteth against the spirit.

St. Paul's doctrine is simple and explicit. Death, he says, reigned over Adam's children, even over those who had not sinned after the likeness of Adam's transgression; agreeing with Moses, who declares God to be one who visits the sins of the fathers on the children, to the third and fourth generation of those who hate Him. But how the sinner will shrink from this message—and shrink the more, the more feeling he is, the less he is wrapped up in selfishness. Yes, that message gives us such a view of the sinfulness of sin as none other can. It tells us why God hates sin with so unextinguishable a hatred, just because He is a God of Love. It is not that man's sin injures God, insults God, as the heathen fancy. Who is God, that man can stir Him up to pride, or wound or disturb His everlasting calm, His self-sufficient perfectness? 'God is tempted of no man,' says St. James.

No. God hates sin. He loves all, and sin harms all; and the sinner may be a torment and a curse, not only to himself, not only to those around him, but to children yet unborn.

This is bad news; and yet sinners must hear it. They must hear it not only put into words by Moses, or by St. Paul, or by any other inspired writer; but they must hear it, likewise, in that perpetual voice of God which we call facts.

Let the sinner who wishes to know what original sin means, and how actual sin in one man breeds original sin in his descendants, look at the world around him, and see. Let him see how St. Paul's doctrine and the doctrine of the Ten Commandments are proved true by experience and by fact: how the past, and how the present likewise, show us whole families, whole tribes, whole aristocracies, whole nations, dwindling down to imbecility, misery, and destruction, because the sins of the fathers are visited on the children.

Physicians, who see children born diseased; born stupid, or even idiotic; born thwart-natured, or passionate, or false, or dishonest, or brutal,—they know well what original sin means, though they call it by their own name of hereditary tendencies. And they know, too, how the sins of a parent, or of a grandparent, or even a great-grandparent, are visited on the children to the third and fourth generation; and they say 'It is a law of nature:' and so it is. But the laws of nature are the laws of God who made her: and His law is the same law by which death reigns even over those who have not sinned after the likeness of Adam; the law by which (even though if Christ be in us, the spirit is life, because of righteousness) the body, nevertheless, is dead, because of sin.

Parents, parents, who hear my words, beware—if not for your own sakes, at least for the sake of your children, and your children's children—lest the wages of your sin should be their death.

And by this time, surely, some of you will be asking, 'What has he said? That there is no escape; that there is no forgiveness?'

None whatsoever, my friends, though you were to cry to heaven for ever and ever, save the one old escape of which you hear in the church every Sunday morning: 'When the wicked man turneth away from his wickedness that he hath committed, and doeth that which is lawful and right, he shall save his soul alive.'

What, does not the blood of Christ cleanse us from all sin?

Yes, from all sin. But not, necessarily, from the wages of all sin.

Judge for yourselves, my friends, again. Listen

to the voice of God revealed in facts. If you, being a drunkard, have injured your constitution by drink, and then are converted, and repent, and turn to God with your whole soul, and become, as you may, if you will, a truly penitent, good, and therefore sober man,— will that cure the disease of your body? It will certainly palliate and ease it: because, instead of being drunken, you will have become sober: but still you will have shortened your days by your past sins; and, in so far, even though the Lord has put away your sin its wages still remain, as death.

So it is, my friends, if you will only believe it, or rather see it with your own eyes, with every sin, and every sort of sin.

You will see, if you look, that the Article speaks exact truth when it says, that the infection of nature doth remain, even in those that are regenerate. It says that of original sin: but it is equally true of actual sin.

Would to God that all men would but believe this, and give up the too common and too dangerous notion, that it is no matter if they go on wrong for a while, provided they come right at last!

No matter? I ask for facts again. Is there a man or woman in this church twenty years old who does not know that it matters? Who does not know that, if they have done wrong in youth, their own wrong deeds haunt them and torment them?—That they are, perhaps the poorer, perhaps the sicklier, perhaps the more ignorant, perhaps the sillier, perhaps the more sorrowful this day, for things which they did twenty, thirty years ago? Is there any one in this church who ever did a wrong thing without smarting for it? If there is (which I question), let him be sure that it is only because his time is not come. Do not fancy that because you are forgiven, you may not be actually less good men all your lives by having sinned when young.

I know it is sometimes said, 'The greater the sinner, the greater the saint.' I do not believe that: because I do not see it. I see, and I thank God for it, that men who have been very wrong at one time, come very right afterwards; that, having found out in earnest that the wages of sin are death, they do repent in earnest, and receive the gift of eternal life through Jesus Christ. But I see, too, that the bad habits, bad passions, bad methods of thought, which they have indulged in youth, remain more or less, and make them worse men, sillier men, less useful men, less happy men, sometimes to their lives' end: and they, if they be true Christians, know it, and repent of their early sins, not once for all only, but all their lives long; because they feel that they have weakened and worsened themselves thereby.

It stands to reason, my friends, that it should be so.

If a man loses his way, and finds it again, he is so much the less forward on his way, surely, by all the time he has spent in getting back into the road. If a child has a violent illness, it stops growing, because the life and nourishment which ought to have gone towards its growth, are spent in curing its disease. And so, if a man has indulged in bad habits in his youth, he is but too likely (let him do what he will) to be a less good man for it to his life's end, because the Spirit of God, which ought to have been making him grow in grace, freely and healthily, to the stature of a perfect man, to the fulness of the measure of Christ, is striving to conquer old bad habits, and cure old diseases of character; and the man, even though he does enter into life, enters into it halt and maimed; and the wages of his sin have been, as they always will be, death to some powers, some faculties of his soul.

Think over these things, my friends; and believe that the wages of sin are death, and that there is no escaping from God's just and everlasting laws. But meanwhile, let us judge no man. This is a great and a solemn reason for observing, with fear and trembling, our Lord's command, for it is nothing less, 'Judge not, and ye shall not be judged; condemn not and ye shall not be condemned.'

For we never can know how much of any man's

misconduct is to be set down to original, and how much to actual, sin;—how much disease of mind and heart he has inherited from his parents, how much he has brought upon himself.

Therefore judge no man, but yourselves. Search your own hearts, to see what manner of men you really wish to be; judge yourselves, lest God should judge you.

Do you wish to go on as you like here on earth, right or wrong, in the hope that, somehow or other, the punishment of your sins will be forgiven you at the last day?

Then know that that is impossible. As a man sows, so shall he reap; and if you sow to the flesh, of the flesh you will reap—corruption. The wages of sin are death. Those wages will be paid you, and you must take them whether you like or not.

But do you wish to be Good? Do you see (I trust in God that many of you do) that goodness is the only wise, safe, prudent life for you: because it is the only path the end of which is not death?

Do you see that goodness is the only right and honourable life for you, because it is the only path by which you can do your duty to man or to God; the only method by which you can show your gratitude to God for all His goodness to you, and can please Him, in return for all that He has done by His grace and free love to bless you?

Do you, in a word, repent you truly of your former sins, and purpose to lead a new life? Then know, that all beyond is the free grace, the free gift of God. You have to earn nothing, to buy nothing. The will is all God asks. Eternal life is the gift of God through Jesus Christ.

Freely He forgives you all your past sins, for the sake of that precious blood which was shed on the cross for the sins of the whole world. Freely He takes you back, as His child, to your Father's house. Freely, He gives you His Holy Spirit, the Spirit of Goodness, the Spirit of Life, to put into your mind good desires, and enable you to bring those desires to good effect, that you may live the eternal life of grace and goodness for ever, whether in earth or heaven.

Yes, it is the Gift of God, which raises you from the death of sin to the life of righteousness; and if you have that gift, you will not murmur, surely, though you have to bear, more or less, the just and natural consequences of your former sins; though you be, through your own guilt, a sadder man to your dying day. Be content. You are forgiven. You are cleansed from your sin; is not that mercy enough? Why are you to demand of God, that He should over and above cleanse you from the consequences of your sin? He may leave them there to trouble and sadden you, just because He loves you, and desires to chasten you, and keep you in mind of what you were, and what you would be again, at any moment, if His Spirit left you to yourself. You may have to enter into life halt and maimed: yet, be content; you have a thousand times more than you deserve, for at least you enter into Life.

SERMON V.

NIGHT AND DAY

(Preached at the Chapel Royal)

ROMANS xiii. 12.

The night is far spent, the day is at hand; let us therefore cast off the works of darkness, and let us put on the armour of light.

CERTAIN commentators would tell us, that St. Paul wrote these words in the expectation that the end of the world, and the second coming of Christ, were very near. The night was far spent, and the day of the Lord at hand. Salvation—deliverance from the destruction impending on the world, was nearer than when his converts first believed. Shortly the Lord would appear in glory, and St. Paul and his converts would be caught up to meet Him in the air.

No doubt St. Paul's words will bear this meaning. No doubt there are many passages in his writings which seem to imply that he thought the end of the world was near; and that Christ would reappear in glory, while he, Paul, was yet alive on the earth. And there are passages, too, which seem to imply that he afterwards altered that opinion, and, no longer expecting to be caught up to meet the Lord in the air, desired to depart himself, and be with Christ, in the consciousness that 'He was ready to be offered up, and the time of his departure was at hand.'

I say that there are passages which seem to imply such a change in St. Paul's opinions. I do not say that they actually imply it. If I had a positive opinion on the matter, I should not be hasty to give it. These questions of 'criticism,' as they are now called, are far less important than men fancy just now. A generation or two hence, it is to be hoped, men will see how very unimportant they are, and will find that they have detracted very little from the authority of Scripture as a whole; and that they have not detracted in the least from the Gospel and good news which Scripture proclaims to men—the news of a perfect God, who will have men to become perfect even as He, their Father in heaven, is perfect; who sent His only begotten Son into the world, that the world through Him might be saved.

In this case, I verily believe, it matters little to us whether St. Paul, when he wrote these words, wrote them under the belief that Christ's second coming was at hand. We must apply to his words the great rule, that no prophecy of Scripture is of any private interpretation—that is, does not apply exclusively to any one fact or event: but fulfils itself again and again, in a hundred unexpected ways, because he who wrote it was moved by the Holy Spirit, who revealed to him the eternal and ever-working laws of the Kingdom of God. Therefore, I say, the words are true for us at this moment. To us, though we have, as far as I can see, not the least reasonable cause for supposing the end of the world to be more imminent than it was a thousand years ago—to us, nevertheless, and to every generation of men, the night is always far spent, and the day is always at hand.

And this, surely, was in the mind of those who appointed this text to be read as the Epistle for the first Sunday in Advent.

Year after year, though Christ has not returned to judgment; though scoffers have been saying, 'Where is the promise of His coming? for all things continue as they were at the beginning'—Year after year, I say, are the clergy bidden to tell the people that the night is far spent, that the day is at hand; and to tell them so, because it is true. Whatsoever St. Paul meant, or did not mean, by the words, a few years after our Lord's ascension into heaven, they are there, for ever, written by one who was moved by the Holy Ghost; and hence they have an eternal moral and spiritual significance to mankind in every age.

Whatever these words may, or may not have meant to St. Paul when he wrote them first, in the prime of life, we may never know, and we need not know. But we can guess surely enough what they must have meant to him in after years, when he could say—as would to God we all might be able to say—

'I have fought a good fight, I have finished my course, I have kept the faith: henceforth there is laid up for me a crown of righteousness, which the Lord, the righteous Judge, shall give me at that day: and not to me only, but unto all them that love His appearing.'

To him, then, the night would surely mean this mortal life on earth. The day would mean the immortal life to come.

For is not this mortal life, compared with that life to come, as night compared with day? I do not mean to speak evil of it. God forbid that we should do anything but thank God for this life. God forbid that we should say impiously to Him, Why hast thou made me thus? No. God made this mortal life, and therefore, like all things which He has made, it is very good. But there are good nights, and there are bad nights; and there are happy lives, and unhappy ones. But what are they at best? What is the life of the happiest man without the Holy Spirit of God? A night full of pleasant dreams. What is the life of the wisest man? A night of darkness, through which he gropes his way by lanthorn-light, slowly, and with many mistakes and stumbles. When we compare man's vast capabilities with his small deeds; when we think how much he might know,—how little he does know in this mortal life,—can we wonder that the highest spirits in every age have looked on death as a deliverance out of darkness and a dungeon? And if this is life at the best, what is life at the worst? To how many is life a night, not of peace and rest, but of tossing and weariness, pain and sickness, anxiety and misery, till they are ready to cry, When will it be over? When will kind Death come and give me rest? When will the night of this life be spent, and the day of God arise? 'Out of the depths have I cried unto thee, O Lord. Lord, hear my voice.... My soul doth wait for the Lord, more than the sick man who watches for the morning.'

Yes, think,—for it is good at times, however happy one may be oneself, to think—of all the misery and sorrow that there is on earth, and how many there are who would be glad to hear that it was nearly over; glad to hear that the night was far spent, and the day was at hand.

And even the happiest ought to 'know the time.' To know that the night is far spent, and the day at hand. To know, too, that the night at best was not given us, to sleep it all through, from sunset to sunrise. No industrious man does that. Either he works after sunset, and often on through the long hours, and into the short hours, before he goes to rest: or else he rises before daybreak, and gets ready for the labours of the coming day. The latter no man can do in this life. For we all sleep away, more or less, the beginning of our life, in the time of childhood. There is no sin in that—God seems to have ordained that so it should be. But, to sleep away our manhood likewise,—is there no sin in that? As we grow older, must we not awake out of sleep, and set to work, to be ready for the day of God which will dawn on us when we pass out of this mortal life into the world to come?

As we grow older, and as we get our share of the cares, troubles, experiences of life, it is high time to wake out of sleep, and ask Christ to give us light—light enough to see our way through the night of this life, till the everlasting day shall dawn.

'Knowing the time;'—the time of this our mortal life. How soon it will be over, at the longest! How short the time seems since we were young! How quickly it has gone! How every year, as we grow older seems to go more and more quickly, and there is less time to do what we want, to think seriously, to improve ourselves. So soon, and it will be over, and we shall have no time at all, for we shall be in eternity. And what then? What then? That depends on what now. On what we are doing now. Are we letting our short span of life slip away in sleep; fancying ourselves all the while wide awake, as we do in dreams—till we wake really; and find that it is daylight, and that all our best dreams were nothing but useless fancy? How many dream away their lives! Some upon gain, some upon pleasure, some upon petty self-interest, petty quarrels, petty ambitions, petty squabbles and jealousies about this person and that, which are no more worthy to take up a reasonable human being's time and thoughts than so many dreams would be. Some, too, dream away their lives in sin, in works of darkness which they are forced for shame and safety to hide, lest they should come to the light and be exposed. So people dream their lives away, and go about their daily business as men who walk in their sleep, wandering about with their eyes open, and yet seeing nothing of what is really around them. Seeing nothing: though they think that they see, and know their own interest, and are shrewd enough to find their way about this world. But they know nothing—nothing of the very world with which they pride themselves they are so thoroughly acquainted. None know less of the world than those who pride themselves on being men of the world. For the true light, which shines all round them, they do not see, and therefore they do not see the truth of things by that light. If they did, then they would see that of which now they do not even dream.

They would see that God was around them, about their path and about their bed, and spying out all their ways; and in the light of His presence, they dare not be frivolous, dare not be ignorant, dare not be mean, dare not be spiteful, dare not be unclean.

They would see that Christ was around them, knocking at the door of their hearts, that He may enter in, and dwell there, and give them peace; crying to their restless, fretful, confused, unhappy souls, 'Come unto Me, all ye that labour and are heavy laden, and I will give you rest. Take My yoke upon you and learn of Me; for I am meek and lowly in heart: and ye shall find rest unto your souls.'

They would see that Duty was around them. Duty —the only thing really worth living for. The only thing which will really pay a man, either for this life or the next. The only thing which will give a man rest and peace, manly and quiet thoughts, a good conscience and a stout heart, in the midst of hard labour, anxiety, sorrow and disappointment: because he feels at least that he is doing his duty; that he is obeying God and Christ, that he is working with them, and for them, and that, therefore, they are working with him, and for him. God, Christ, and Duty—these, and more, will a man see if he will awake out of sleep, and consider where he is, by the light of God's Holy Spirit.

Then will that man feel that he must cast away the works of darkness; whether of the darkness of foul and base sins; or the darkness of envy, spite, and revenge; or the mere darkness of ignorance and silliness, thoughtlessness and frivolity. He must cast them away, he will see. They will not succeed—they are not safe—in such a serious world as this. The term of this mortal life is too short, and too awfully important, to be spent in such dreams as these. The man is too awfully near to God, and to Christ, to dare to play the fool in their Divine presence. This earth looks to him, now that he sees it in the true light, one great temple of God, in which he dare not, for very shame, misbehave himself. He must cast away the works of darkness, and put on the armour of light, now in the time of this mortal life; lest, when Christ comes in His glory to judge the quick and the dead, he be found asleep, dreaming, useless, unfit for the eternal world to come.

Then let him awake, and cry to Christ for light: and Christ will give him light—enough, at least, to see his way through the darkness of this life, to that eternal life of which it is written, 'They need no candle there, nor light of the sun: for the Lord God and the Lamb are the light thereof.' And he will find that the armour of light is an armour indeed. A defence against all enemies, a helmet for his head, and breastplate for his heart, against all that can really harm his mind or soul.

If a man, in the struggle of life, sees God, and Christ, and Duty, all around him, that thought will be a helmet for his head. It will keep his brain and mind clear, quiet, prudent to perceive and know what things he ought to do. It will give him that Divine wisdom, of which Solomon says, in his Proverbs, that the beginning of wisdom is the fear of the Lord.

The light will give him, I say, judgment and wisdom to perceive what he ought to do; and it will give him, too, grace and power faithfully to fulfil the same. For it will be a breastplate to his heart. It will keep his heart sound, as well as his head. It will save him from breaking his good resolutions, and from deserting his duty out of cowardice, or out of passion. The light of Christ will keep his heart pure, unselfish, forgiving; ready to hope all things, believe all things, endure all things, by that Divine charity which God will pour into his soul.

For when he looks at things in the light of Christ, what does he see? Christ hanging on the cross, praying for His murderers, dying for the sins of the whole world. And what does the light which streams from that cross show him of Christ? That the likeness of Christ is summed up in one word—self-sacrificing love. What does the light which streams from that cross show him of the world and mankind, in spite of all their sins? That they belong to Him who died for them, and bought them with His own most precious blood.

'Beloved, herein is love indeed. Not that we loved God, but that He loved us, and sent His Son to be the propitiation of our sins.'

'Beloved, if God so loved us, we ought also to love one another.'

After that sight a man cannot hate; cannot revenge He must forgive; he must love. From hence he is in the light, and sees his duty and his path through life. 'For he that hateth his brother walketh in darkness, and knoweth not whither he goeth: because darkness has blinded his eyes. But he that loveth his brother abideth in the light, and there is no occasion of stumbling in him. For he who dwelleth in love, dwelleth in God, and God in him.'

Therefore cast away the works of darkness, and put you on the armour of light, and be good men and true.

For of this the Holy Ghost prophesies by the mouth of St. Paul, and of all apostles and prophets. Not of times and seasons, which God the Father has kept in His own hand: not of that day and hour of which no man knows; no, not the Angels in heaven, neither the Son; but the Father only: not of these does the Holy Ghost testify to men. Not of chronology, past or future: but of holiness; because he is a Holy Spirit.

For this purpose God, the Holy Father, sent His Son into the world. For this God, the Holy Son, died upon the cross. For this God, the Holy Ghost—proceeding from both the Father and the Son—inspired prophets and apostles; that they might teach men to cast away the works of darkness, and put on the armour of light; and become holy, as God is holy; pure, as God is pure; true, as God is true; and good, as God is good.

SERMON VI.

THE SHAKING OF THE HEAVENS AND THE EARTH.

(Preached at the Chapel Royal, Whitehall.)

HEBREWS xii. 26—29.

But now he hath promised, saying, Yet once more I shake not the earth only, but also heaven. And this word, Yet once more, signifieth the removing of those things that are shaken, as of things that are made, that those things which cannot be shaken may remain. Wherefore, we receiving a kingdom which cannot be moved, let us have grace, whereby we may serve God acceptably with reverence and godly fear: for our God is a consuming fire.

THIS is one of the Royal texts of the New Testament. It declares one of those great laws of the kingdom of God, which may fulfil itself, once and again, at many eras, and by many methods; which fulfilled itself especially and most gloriously in the first century after Christ; which fulfilled itself again in the fifth century; and again at the time of the Crusades; and again at the great Reformation in the sixteenth century; and is fulfilling itself again at this very day.

Now, in our fathers' time, and in our own unto this day, is the Lord Christ shaking the heavens and the earth, that those things which are made may be removed, and that those things which cannot be shaken may remain. We all confess this fact, in different phrases. We say that we live in an age of change, of transition, of scientific and social revolution. Our notions of the physical universe are rapidly altering with the new discoveries of science; and our notions of Ethics and Theology are altering as rapidly.

The era looks differently to different minds, just as the first century after Christ looked differently, according as men looked with faith towards the future, or with regret towards the past. Some rejoice in the present era as one of progress. Others lament over it as one of decay. Some say that we are on the eve of a Reformation, as great and splendid as that of the sixteenth century. Others say that we are rushing headlong into scepticism and atheism. Some say that a new era is dawning on humanity; others that the world and the Church are coming to an end, and the last day is at hand. Both parties may be right, and both may be wrong. Men have always talked thus at great crises. They talked thus in the first century, in the fifth, in the eleventh, in the sixteenth. And then both parties were right, and yet both wrong. And why not now? What they meant to say, and what they mean to say now, is what he who wrote the Epistle to the Hebrews said for them long ago in far deeper, wider, more accurate words—that the Lord Christ was shaking the heavens and the earth, that those things which can be shaken may be removed, as things which are made—cosmogonies, systems, theories, fashions, prejudices, of man's invention: while those things which cannot be shaken may remain, because they are eternal, the creation not of man, but of God.

'Yet once more I shake not the earth only, but also heaven.' Not merely the physical world, and man's conceptions thereof, but the spiritual world, and man's conceptions of that likewise.

How have our conceptions of the physical world been shaken of late, with ever-increasing violence! How simple, and easy, and certain, it all looked to our forefathers! How complex, how uncertain, it looks to us! With increased knowledge has come—not increased doubt—that I deny; but increased reverence; increased fear of rash assertions, increased awe of facts, as the acted words and thoughts of God. Once for all, I deny that this age is an irreverent one. I say that an irreverent age is an age like the Middle Age, in which men dared to fancy that they could and did know all about earth and heaven; and set up their petty cosmogonies, their petty systems of doctrine, as measures of the ways of that God whom the heaven, and the heaven of heavens, cannot contain.

It was simple enough, their theory of the universe. The earth was a flat plain; for did not the earth look flat? Or if some believed the earth to be a globe, yet the existence of antipodes was an unscriptural heresy. Above were the heavens: first the lower heavens in which the stars were fixed and moved; and above them heaven after heaven, each peopled of higher orders, up to that heaven of heavens in which Deity—and by Him, the Mother of Deity—were enthroned.

And below—What could be more clear, more certain, than this—that as above the earth was the kingdom of light, and joy, and holiness, so below the earth was the kingdom of darkness, and torment, and sin? What could be more certain? Had not even the heathens said so, by the mouth of the poet Virgil? What could be more simple, rational, orthodox, than to adopt (as they actually did) Virgil's own words, and talk of Tartarus, Styx, and Phlegethon, as indisputable Christian entities. They were not aware that the Buddhists of the far East had held much the same theory of endless retribution several centuries before; and that Dante, with his various *bolge*, tenanted each by its various species of sinners, was merely re-echoing the horrors which are to be seen painted on the walls of any Buddhist temple, as they were on the walls of so many European churches during the Middle Ages, when men really believed in that same Tartarology, with the same intensity with which they now believe in the conclusions of astronomy or of chemistry.

To them, indeed, it was all an indisputable or physical fact, as any astronomic or chemical fact would have been; for they saw it with their own eyes.

Virgil had said that the mouth of Tartarus was there in Italy, by the volcanic lake of Avernus; and after the first eruption of Vesuvius in the first century, nothing seemed more probable. Etna, Stromboli, Hecla, must be, likewise, all mouths of hell; and there were not wanting holy hermits who had heard within those craters, shrieks and clanking chains, and the shouts of demons tormenting endlessly the souls of the lost. And now, how has all this been shaken? How much of all this does any educated man, though he be pious, though he desire with all his heart to be orthodox—and is orthodox in fact—how much of all this does he believe, as he believes that the earth is round, or, that if he steals his neighbour's goods he commits a crime?

For, since these days, the earth has been shaken, and with it the heavens likewise, in that very sense in which the expression is used in the text. Our conceptions of them have been shaken. The Copernican system shook them, when it told men that the earth was but a tiny globular planet revolving round the sun. Geology shook them, when it told men that the earth has endured for countless ages, during which whole continents have been submerged, whole seas become dry land, again and again. Even now the heavens and the earth are being shaken by researches into the antiquity of the human race, and into the origin and the mutability of species, which, issue in what results they may, will shake for us, meanwhile, theories which are venerable with the authority of nearly eighteen hundred years, and of almost every great Doctor since St. Augustine.

And as our conception of the physical universe has been shaken, the old theory of a Tartarus beneath the earth has been shaken also, till good men have been glad to place Tartarus in a comet, or in the sun, or to welcome the possible, but unproved hypothesis, of a central fire in the earth's core, not on any scientific grounds, but if by any means a spot may be found in space corresponding to that of which Virgil, Dante, and Milton sang.

And meanwhile—as was to be expected from a generation which abhors torture, labours for the reformation of criminals, and even doubts whether it should not abolish capital punishment—a shaking of the heavens is abroad, of which we shall hear more and more, as the years roll on—a general inclination to ask whether

Holy Scripture really endorses the Middle-age notions of future punishment in endless torment? Men are writing and speaking on this matter, not merely with ability and learning, but with a piety, and reverence for Scripture which (rightly or wrongly employed) must, and will, command attention. They are saying that it is not those who deny these notions who disregard the letter of Scripture, but those who assert them; that they are distorting the plain literal text, in order to make Scripture fit the writings of Dante and Milton, when they translate into 'endless torments after death,' such phrases as the outer darkness, the undying worm, the Gehenna of fire—which manifestly (say these men), if judged by fair rules of interpretation, refer to this life, and specially to the fate of the Jewish nation: or when they tell us that eternal death means really eternal life, only in torments. We demand, they say, not a looser, but a stricter; not a more metaphoric, but a more literal; not a more careless, but a more reverent interpretation of Scripture; and whether this demand be right or wrong, it will not pass unheard.

And even more severely shaken, meanwhile, is that mediæval conception of heaven and hell, by the question which educated men are asking more and more:— 'Heaven and hell—the spiritual world—Are they merely invisible places in space, which may become visible hereafter? or are they not rather the moral world—the world of right and wrong? Love and righteousness—is not that the heaven itself wherein God dwells? Hatred and sin—is not that hell itself, wherein dwells all that is opposed to God?'

And out of that thought, right or wrong, other thoughts have sprung—of ethics, of moral retribution—not new at all (say these men), but to be found in Scripture, and in the writings of all great Christian divines, when they have listened, not to systems, but to the voice of their own hearts.

'We do not deny' (they say) 'that the wages of sin are death. We do not deny the necessity of punishment—the certainty of punishment. We see it working awfully enough around us in this life; we believe that it may work in still more awful forms in the life to come. Only tell us not that it must be endless, and thereby destroy its whole purpose, and (as we think) its whole morality. We, too, believe in an eternal fire; but we believe its existence to be, not a curse, but a Gospel and a blessing, seeing that that fire is God Himself, who taketh away the sins of the world, and of whom it is therefore written, Our God is a consuming fire.'

Questions, too, have arisen, of—'What *is* moral retribution? Should punishment have any end but the good of the offender? Is God so controlled that He must needs send into the world beings whom He knows to be incorrigible, and doomed to endless misery?

And if not so controlled, then is not the other alternative as to His character more fearful still? Does He not bid us copy Him, His justice, His love? Then is that His justice, is that His love, which if we copied we should be unjust and unloving utterly? Are there two moralities, one for God, and quite another for man, made in the image of God? Can these dark dogmas be true of a Father who bids us be perfect as He is, in that He sends His sun to shine on the evil and the good, and His rain on the just and unjust? Or of a Son who so loved the world that He died to save the world:—and surely not in vain?'

These questions—be they right or wrong—educated men and women of all classes and denominations—orthodox, be it remembered, as well as unorthodox—are asking, and will ask more and more, till they receive an answer. And if we of the clergy cannot give them an answer which accords with their conscience and their reason; if we tell them that the words of Scripture, and the integral doctrines of Christianity, demand the same notions of moral retribution as were current in the days when men racked criminals, burned heretics alive, and believed that every Mussulman whom they slaughtered in a crusade went straight to endless torments,—then evil times will come, both for the clergy and the Christian religion, for many a year henceforth.

What then are we to believe? What are we to do, amid this shaking of the earth and heaven? Are we to degenerate into a lazy and heartless scepticism, which, under pretence of liberality and charity, believes that everything is a little true, everything is a little false—in one word, believes nothing at all? Or are we to degenerate into unmanly and faithless wailings, crying out that the flood of infidelity is irresistible, that the last days are come, and that Christ has deserted His Church?

Not if we will believe the text. The text tells us of something which cannot be moved, though all around it reel and crumble—of a firm standing-ground, which would endure, though the heavens should pass away as a scroll, and the earth should be removed, and cast into the midst of the sea.

We have a kingdom, the Scripture says, which cannot be moved, even the kingdom of Him whom it calls shortly after 'Jesus Christ, the same yesterday, to-day and for ever.' An eternal and unchangeable kingdom, ruled by an eternal and unchangeable King. That is what cannot be moved.

Scripture does not say that we have an unchangeable cosmogony, an unchangeable theory of moral retribution, an unchangeable system of dogmatic propositions. Whether we have, or have not, it is not of them that Scripture reminds the Jews, when the heavens and the earth were shaken; when their own nation and worship were in their death-agony, and all the beliefs and practices of men were in a whirl of doubt and confusion, of decay and birth side by side, such as the world had never seen before. Not of them does it remind the Jews, but of the changeless kingdom, and the changeless King.

My friends, lay it seriously to heart, once and for all. Do you believe that you are subjects of that kingdom, and that Christ is the living, ruling, guiding King thereof? Whatsoever Scripture does not say, Scripture speaks of that, again and again, in the plainest terms. But do you believe it? These are days in which the preacher ought to ask every man whether he believes it, and bid him, of whatever else he repents of, to repent, at least, of not having believed this primary doctrine (I may almost say) of Scripture and of Christianity.

But if you do believe it, will it seem strange to you to believe this also,—That, considering who Christ is, the co-eternal and co-equal Son of God, He may be actually governing His kingdom; and if so, that He may know better how to govern it than such poor worms as we? That if the heavens and the earth be shaken, Christ Himself may be shaking them? if opinions be changing, Christ Himself may be changing them? If new truths and facts are being discovered, Christ Himself may be revealing them? That if those truths seem to contradict the truths which He has already taught us, they do not really contradict them, any more than those reasserted in the sixteenth century? That if our God be a consuming fire, He is now burning up (to use St. Paul's parable) the chaff and stubble which men have built on the one foundation of Christ, that, at last, nought but the pure gold may remain? Is it not possible? Is it not most probable, if we only believe that Christ is a real, living King, an active, practical King,—who, with boundless wisdom and skill, love and patience, is educating and guiding Christendom, and through Christendom the whole human race?

If men would but believe that, how different would be their attitude toward new facts, toward new opinions! They would receive them with grace; gracefully, courteously, fairly, charitably, and with that reverence and godly fear which the text tells us is the way to serve God acceptably. They would say: 'Christ (so the Scripture tells us) has been educating man through Abraham, through Moses, through David, through the Jewish prophets, through the Greeks, through the Romans; then through Himself, as man as well as God; and after His ascension, through His Apostles, especially through St. Paul, to an ever-increasing understanding of God, and the universe, and themselves. And even after their time He did not cease His education. Why should He? How could He, who said of

Himself, "All power is given to me in heaven and earth;" "Lo, I am with you alway to the end of the world;" and again, "My Father worketh hitherto, and I work?"

'At the Reformation in the sixteenth century He called on our forefathers to repent—that is, to change their minds—concerning opinions which had been undoubted for more than a thousand years. Why should He not be calling on us at this time likewise? And if any answer, that the Reformation was only a return to the primitive faith of the Apostles—Why should not this shaking of the hearts and minds of men issue in a still further return, in a further correction of errors, a further sweeping away of additions, which are not integral to the Christian creeds, but which were left behind, through natural and necessary human frailty, by our great Reformers? Wise they were,—good and great,—as giants on the earth, while we are but as dwarfs; but, as the hackneyed proverb tells us, the dwarf on the giant's shoulders may see further than the giant himself.'

Ah! that men would approach new truth in that spirit; in the spirit of godly fear, which is inspired by the thought that we are in the kingdom of God, and that the King thereof is Christ, both God and man, once crucified for us, now living for us for ever! Ah! that they would thus serve God, waiting, as servants before a lord, for the slightest sign which might intimate his will! Then they would look at new truths with caution; in that truly conservative spirit which is the duty of all Christians, and the especial strength of the Englishman. With caution,—lest in grasping eagerly after what is new, we throw away truth which we have already: but with awe and reverence; for Christ may have sent the new truth; and he who fights against it, may haply be found fighting against God. And so would they indeed obey the Apostolic injunction— Prove all things, hold fast that which is good,—that which is pure, fair, noble, tending to the elevation of men; to the improvement of knowledge, justice, mercy, well-being; to the extermination of ignorance, cruelty, and vice. That, at least, must come from Christ, unless the Pharisees were right when they said that evil spirits could be cast out by Beelzebub, prince of the devils.

How much more Christian, reverent, faithful, as well as more prudent, rational, and philosophical, would such a temper be than that which condemns all changes *à priori*, at the first hearing, or rather, too often, without any hearing at all, in rage and terror, like that of the animal who at the same moment barks at, and runs away from, every unknown object.

At least that temper of mind will give us calm; faith, patience, hope, charity, though the heavens and the earth are shaken around us. For we have received a kingdom which cannot be moved, and in the King thereof we have the most perfect trust: for us He stooped to earth, was born, and died on the cross; and can we not trust Him? Let Him do what He will; let Him teach us what He will; let Him lead us whither He will. Wherever He leads, we shall find pasture. Wherever He leads, must be the way of truth, and we will follow, and say, as Socrates of old used to say, Let us follow the Logos boldly, whithersoever it leadeth. If Socrates had courage to say it, how much more should we, who know what he, good man, knew not, that the Logos is not a mere argument, train of thought, necessity of logic, but a Person—perfect God and perfect man, even Jesus Christ, 'the same yesterday, to day, and for ever,' who promised of old, and therefore promises to us, and our children after us, to lead those who trust Him into all truth.

SERMON VII.

THE BATTLE OF LIFE.

GALATIANS v. 16, 17.

I say then, Walk in the Spirit, and ye shall not fulfil the lust of the flesh. For the flesh lusteth against the Spirit, and the Spirit against the flesh: so that ye cannot do the things that ye would.

A GREAT poet speaks of 'Happiness, our being's end and aim;' and he has been reproved for so doing. Men have said, and wisely, the end and aim of our being is not happiness, but goodness. If goodness comes first, then happiness may come after. But if not, something better than happiness may come, even blessedness.

This it is, I believe, which our Lord may have meant when He said, 'He that saveth his life, or soul' (for the two words in Scripture mean exactly the same thing), 'shall lose it. And he that loseth his life, shall save it. For what is a man profited if he gain the whole world, and lose his own life?'

How is this? It is a hard saying. Difficult to believe, on account of the natural selfishness which lies deep in all of us. Difficult even to understand in these days, when religion itself is selfish, and men learn more and more to think that the end and aim of religion is not to make them good while they live, but merely to save their souls after they die.

But whether it be hard to understand or not, we must understand it, if we would be good men. And how to understand it, the Epistle for this day will teach us.

'Walk in the Spirit, and ye shall not fulfil the lust of the flesh.' The Spirit, which is the Spirit of God within our hearts and conscience, says—Be good. The flesh, the animal, savage nature, which we all have in common with the dumb animals, says—Be happy. Please yourself. Do what you like. Eat and drink, for to-morrow you die.

But, happily for us, the Spirit lusts against the flesh. It draws us the opposite way. It lifts us up, instead of dragging us down. It has nobler aims, higher longings. It, as St. Paul puts it, will not let us do the things that we would. It will not let us do just what we like, and please ourselves. It often makes us unhappy just when we try to be happy. It shames us, and cries in our hearts—You were not meant merely to please yourselves, and be as the beasts which perish.

But how few listen to that voice of God's Spirit within their hearts, though it be just the noblest thing of which they will ever be aware on earth!

How few listen to it, till the lusts of the flesh are worn out, and have worn them out likewise, and made them reap the fruit which they have sowed—sowing to the selfish flesh, and of the selfish flesh reaping corruption.

The young man says—I will be happy and do what I like; and runs after what he calls pleasure. The middle-aged man, grown more prudent, says—I will be happy yet, and runs after money, comfort, fame and power. But what do they gain? 'The works of the flesh,' the fruit of this selfish lusting after mere earthly happiness, 'are manifest, which are these:'—not merely that open vice and immorality into which the young man falls when he craves after mere animal pleasure, but 'hatred, variance, emulations, wrath, strife, seditions, heresies'—*i.e.*, factions in Church or State—'envyings, murders, and such like.'

Thus men put themselves under the law. Not under Moses' law, of course, but under some law or other.

For why has law been invented? Why is it needed, with all its expense? Law is meant to prevent, if possible, men harming each other by their own selfishness, by those lusts of the flesh which tempt every man to seek his own happiness, careless of his neighbour's happiness, interest, morals; by all the passions which make men their own tormentors, and which make the history of every nation too often a history of crime, and folly, and faction, and war, sad and shameful to read; all those passions of which St. Paul says once and for ever, that those who do such things 'shall not inherit the kingdom of God.'

These are the sad consequences of giving way to the flesh, the selfish animal nature within us: and most miserable would man be if that were all he had to look to. Miserable, were there not a kingdom of God, into which he could enter all day long, and be at peace; and a Spirit of God, who would raise him up to the spiritual life of love, joy, peace, long-suffering, gentleness, goodness, faith, meekness, temperance; and a Son of God, the King of that kingdom, the Giver of that Spirit, who cries for ever to every one of us—'Come unto Me, ye that are weary and heavy laden, and I will give you rest. Take My yoke on you, and learn of Me, for I am meek and lowly of heart; and ye shall find rest unto your souls.'

Love, joy, peace, long-suffering, gentleness, goodness, faith, meekness, temperance; these are the fruits of the Spirit: the spirit of unselfishness; the spirit of charity; the spirit of justice; the spirit of purity; the Spirit of God. Against them there is no law. He who is guided by this Spirit, and he only, may do what he would; for he will wish to do nought but what is right. He is not under the law, but under grace; and full of grace will he be in all his words and works. He has entered into the kingdom of God, and is living therein as God's subject, obeying the royal law of liberty —'Thou shalt love thy neighbour as thyself.'

'The flesh lusteth against the Spirit, and the Spirit against the flesh, so that ye cannot do the things that ye would,' says St. Paul.

My friends, this is the battle of life.

In every one of us, more or less, this battle is going on; a battle between the flesh and the Spirit, between the animal nature and the divine grace. In every one of us, I say, who is not like the heathen, dead in trespasses and sins; in every one of us who has a conscience, excusing or else accusing us. There are those—a very few, I hope—who are sunk below that state; who have lost their sense of right and wrong; who only care to fulfil the lusts of the flesh in pleasure, ease, and vanity. There are those in whom the voice of conscience is dead for a while, silenced by self-conceit; who say in their prosperity, like the foolish Laodiceans, 'I am rich, and increased with goods, and have need of nothing,' and know not that in fact and reality, and in the sight of God, they are 'wretched, and miserable, and poor, and blind, and naked.'

Happy, happy for any and all of us,—if ever we fall into that dream of pride and false security,—to be awakened again, however painful the awakening may be! Happy for every man that the battle between the Spirit and the flesh should begin in him again and again, as long as his flesh is not subdued to his spirit. If he be wrong, the greatest blessing which can happen to him is, that he should find himself in the wrong. If he have been deceiving himself, the greatest blessing is, that God should anoint his eyes that he may see—see himself as he is; see his own inbred corruption; see the sin which doth so easily beset him, whatever it may be. Whatever anguish of mind it may cost him, it is a light price to pay for the inestimable treasure which true repentance and amendment brings; the fine gold of solid self-knowledge, tried in the fire of bitter experience; the white raiment of a pure and simple heart; the eye-salve of honest self-condemnation and noble shame. If he have but these—and these God will give him, in answer to prayer, the prayer of a broken and a contrite heart—then he will be able to carry on the battle against the corrupt flesh, with its affections and lusts, in hope. In the assured hope of final victory. 'For greater is He that is with us, than he that is against us.' He that is against us is our self, our selfish self, our animal nature; and He that is with us is God; God and none other: and who can pluck us out of His hand?

My friends, the bread and the wine on that table are God's own sign to us that He will not leave us to be, like the savage, the slaves of our own animal natures; that He will feed not merely our bodies with animal, but our souls with spiritual food; giving us strength to rise above our selfish selves; and so subdue the flesh to the Spirit, that at last, however long and weary the fight, however sore wounded and often worsted we may be, we shall conquer in the battle of life.

SERMON VIII.

FREE GRACE.

(*Preached before the Queen at Windsor, March* 12, 1865.)

ISAIAH lv. 1.

Ho, every one that thirsteth, come ye to the waters, and he that hath no money; come ye, buy, and eat; yea, come, buy wine and milk without money and without price.

EVERY one who knows his Bible as he should, knows well this noble chapter. It seems to be one of the separate poems or hymns of which the Book of Isaiah is composed. It is certainly one of the most beautiful of them, and also one of the deepest. So beautiful is it, that the good men of old who translated the Bible into English, could not help catching the spirit of the words as they went on with their work, and making the chapter almost a hymn in English, as it is a hymn in Hebrew. Even the very sound of the words, as we listen to them, is a song in itself; and there is perhaps no more perfect piece of writing in the English language, than the greater part of this chapter.

This may not seem a very important matter; and yet

those good men of old must have felt that there was something in this chapter which went home especially to their hearts, and would go home to the hearts of us for whose sake they translated it.

And those good men judged rightly. The care which they bestowed on Isaiah's words has not been in vain. The noble sound of the text has caught many a man's ears, in order that the noble meaning of the text might touch his heart, and bring him back again to God, to seek Him while He may be found, and call on Him while He is near; that so the wicked might forsake his way, and the unrighteous man his thoughts, and return to God, for He will have compassion, and to our God, for He will abundantly pardon; and that he might find that God's thoughts are not as man's thoughts, nor His ways as man's ways, saith the Lord; for as the heavens are higher than the earth, so are His ways and thoughts higher than ours.

Yes—I believe that the beauty of this chapter has made many a man listen to it, who had perhaps never cared to listen to any good before; and learn a precious lesson from it, which he could learn nowhere save in the Bible.

For this text is one of those which have been called the Evangelical Prophecies, in which the prophet rises far above Moses' old law, and the letter of it, which, as St. Paul says, is a letter which killeth; and the spirit of it, which is a spirit which, as St. Paul says, gendereth to bondage and slavish dread of God: an utterance in which the prophet sees by faith the Lord Jesus Christ and His free grace revealed—dimly, of course, and in a figure—but still revealed by the Spirit of God, who spake by the prophets. As St. Paul says, Moses' law made nothing perfect, and therefore had to be disannulled for its unprofitableness and weakness, and a better hope brought in, by which we draw near to God. And here, in this text, we see the better hope coming in, and as it were dawning upon men—the dawn of the Sun of Righteousness, Jesus Christ our Lord, who was to rise afterwards, to be a light to lighten the Gentiles, and the glory of His people Israel.

And what was this better hope? One, St. Paul says, by which we could draw nigh to God; come near to Him; as to a Father, a Saviour, a Comforter, a liege lord—not a tyrant who holds us against our will as his slaves, but a liege lord who holds us with our will as His tenants, His vassals, His liege men, as the good old English words were; one who will take His vassals into His counsel, and inform them with His Spirit, and teach them His mind, that they may do His will and copy His example, and be treated by Him as His friends—in spite of the infinite difference of rank between them and Him, which they must never forget.

But though the difference of rank be infinite and

boundless—for it is the difference between sinful man and God perfect for ever—yet still man can now draw near to God. He is not commanded to stand afar off in fear and trembling, as the old Jews were at Sinai. We have not come, says St. Paul, to a mount which burned with fire, and blackness, and darkness, and storm, and the sound of a trumpet, and the voice of words, which those who heard entreated that they should not be spoken to them any more: for they could not endure that which was commanded: but we are come to the city of the living God, the heavenly Jerusalem, and to the Church of the first-born which are written in heaven, and to God the Judge of all, and to the spirits of just men made perfect, and to Jesus the Mediator of the new covenant, and to the blood of sprinkling.

We are come to God, the Judge of all, and to Christ —not bidden to stand afar off from them. That is the point to which I wish you to attend. For this agrees with the words of the text, 'Ho, every one that thirsteth, come ye to the waters.'

This message it is, which made this chapter precious in the eyes of the good men of old. This message it is, which has made it precious, in all times, to thousands of troubled, hard-worked, weary, afflicted hearts. This is what has made it precious to thousands who were wearied with the burden of their sins, and longed to be made righteous and good; and knew bitterly well that they could not make themselves good, but that God alone could do that; and so longed to come to God, that they might be made good: but did not know whether they might come or not; or whether, if they came, God would receive them, and help them, and convert them. This message it is, which has made the text an evangelical prophecy, to be fulfilled only in Christ—a message which tells men of a God who says, Come. Of a God whom Moses' law, saying merely, 'Thou shalt not,' did not reveal to us, divine and admirable as it was, and is, and ever will be. Of a God whom natural religion, such as even the heathen, St. Paul says, may gain from studying God's works in this wonderful world around us—of a God, I say, whom natural religion does not reveal to us, divine and admirable as it is. But of a God who was revealed, step by step, to the Psalmists and the Prophets, more and more clearly as the years went on; of a God who was fully and utterly revealed, not merely by, but in Jesus Christ our Lord, who was Himself that God, very God of very God begotten, being the brightness of His Father's glory, and the express image of His person; whose message and call, from the first day of His ministry to His glorious ascension, was, Come.

Come unto me, ye that are weary and heavy laden, and I will refresh you.

Come unto Me, and take My yoke on you : for My yoke is easy, and My burden is light.

I am the bread of life. He that cometh to Me shall never hunger, and he that believeth in Me shall never thirst.

All that the Father hath given Me shall come unto Me. And he that cometh to Me I will in no wise cast out.

Nay, the very words of this prophecy Christ took to Himself again and again, speaking of Himself as the fountain of life, health and light; when He stood and cried, saying, If any man thirst, let him come to Me, and drink.

Come unto Me, that ye may have life, is the message of Jesus Christ, both God and man. Come, that you may have forgiveness of your sins; come, that you may have the Holy Spirit, by which you may sin no more, but live the life of the Spirit, the everlasting life of goodness, by which the spirits of just men, and angels, and archangels, live for ever before God.

And what says St. Paul? See that ye refuse not Him that speaketh. For if they escaped not, who refused Him that spake on earth, much more shall not we escape, if we turn away from Him that speaketh from heaven.

Yes. The goodness of God, the condescension of God, instead of making it more easy for sinners to escape, makes it, if possible, more difficult. There are those who fancy that because God is merciful—because it is written in this very chapter, Let a man return to the Lord, and He will have mercy; and to our God, for He will abundantly pardon,—that, therefore, God is indulgent, and will overlook their sins; forgetting that in the verse before it is said, Let the wicked forsake his ways, and the unrighteous man his thoughts, and then —but not till then—let him return to God, to be received with compassion and forgiveness.

Too many know not, as St. Paul says, that the goodness of God leads men, not to sin freely and carelessly without fear of punishment, but leads them to repentance. And yet do not our own hearts and consciences tell us that it is so? That it is more base, and more presumptuous likewise, to turn away from one who speaks with love, than one who speaks with sternness; from one who calls us to come to him, with boundless condescension, than from one who bids us stand afar off and tremble?

Those Jews of old, when they refused to hear God speaking in the thunders of Sinai, committed folly. We, if we refuse to hear God speaking in the tender words of Jesus crucified for us, commit an equal folly: but we commit baseness and ingratitude likewise. They rebelled against a Master: we rebel against a Father.

But, though we deny Him, He cannot deny Himself. We may be false to Him, false to our better selves, false to our baptismal vows: but He cannot be false. He cannot change. He is the same yesterday, to-day, and for ever. What He said on earth, that He says eternally in heaven: If any man thirst, let him come to Me and drink.

Eternally, and for ever, in heaven, says St. John, Christ says, and is, and does, what Isaiah prophesied that He would say, and be, and do,—I am the root and offspring of David, and the bright and morning star. And the Spirit and the Bride (His Spirit and His Church) say, Come. And let him that is athirst, Come: and whosoever will, let him take of the water of life freely. For ever He calls to every anxious soul, every afflicted soul, every weary soul, every discontented soul, to every man who is ashamed of himself, and angry with himself, and longs to live a soberer, gentler, nobler, purer, truer, more useful life—Come. Let him who hungers and thirsts after righteousness, come to the waters; and he that hath no silver—nothing to give to God in return for all His bounty—let him buy without silver, and eat; and live for ever that eternal life of righteousness, holiness, and peace, and joy in the Holy Spirit, which is the one true and only salvation bought for us by the precious blood of Christ, our Lord.

SERMON IX.

EZEKIEL'S VISION.

(Preached before the Queen at Windsor, June 26, 1864.)

EZEKIEL i. 1, 26.

Now it came to pass, as I was among the captives by the river of Chebar, that the heavens were opened, and I saw visions of God. And upon the likeness of the throne was the likeness as the appearance of a man.

EZEKIEL'S Vision may seem to some a strange and unprofitable subject on which to preach. It ought not to be so in fact. All Scripture is given by inspiration of God, and is profitable for teaching, for correction, for reproof, for instruction in righteousness. And so will this Vision be to us, if we try to understand it aright. We shall find in it fresh knowledge of God, a clearer and fuller revelation, made to Ezekiel, than had been, up to his time, made to any man.

I am well aware that there are some very difficult verses in the text. It is difficult, if not impossible, to understand exactly what presented itself to Ezekiel's mind.

Ezekiel saw a whirlwind come out of the north; a whirling globe of fire; four living creatures coming out of the midst thereof. So far the imagery is simple enough, and grand enough. But when he begins to speak of the living creatures, the cherubim, his description is very obscure. All that we discover is, a vision of huge creatures with the feet, and (as some think) the body of an ox, with four wings, and four faces,—those of a man, an ox, a lion, and an eagle. Ezekiel seems to discover afterwards that these are the cherubim, the same which overshadowed the ark in Moses' tabernacle and Solomon's temple—only of a more complex form; for Moses' and Solomon's cherubim are believed to have had but one face each, while Ezekiel's had four.

Now, concerning the cherubim, and what they meant, we know very little. The Jews, at the time of the fall of Jerusalem, had forgotten their meaning. Josephus, indeed, says they had forgotten their very shape.

Some light has been thrown, lately, on the figures of these creatures, by the sculptures of those very Assyrian cities to which Ezekiel was a captive,—those huge winged oxen and lions with human heads; and those huge human figures with four wings each, let down and folded round them just as Ezekiel describes, and with heads, sometimes of the lion, and sometimes of the eagle. None, however, have been found as yet, I believe, with four faces, like those of Ezekiel's Vision; they are all of the simpler form of Solomon's cherubim. But there is little doubt that these sculptures were standing there perfect in Ezekiel's time, and that he and the Jews who were captive with him may have seen them often. And there is little doubt also what these figures meant: that they were symbolic of royal spirits —those 'thrones, dominations, princedoms, powers,' of which Milton speaks,—the powers of the earth and heaven, the royal archangels who, as the Chaldæans believed, governed the world, and gave it and all things life; symbolized by them under the types of the four royal creatures of the world, according to the Eastern nations; the ox signifying labour, the lion power, the eagle foresight, and the man reason.

So with the wheels which Ezekiel sees. We find them in the Assyrian sculptures—wheels with a living spirit sitting in each, a human figure with outspread wings; and these seem to have been the genii, or guardian angels, who watched over their kings, and gave them fortune and victory.

For these Chaldæans were specially worshippers of angels and spirits; and they taught the Jews many notions about angels and spirits, which they brought home with them into Judæa after the captivity.

Of them, of course, we read little or nothing in Holy Scripture; but there is much, and too much, about them in the writings of the old Rabbis, the Scribes and Pharisees of the New Testament.

Now Ezekiel, inspired by the Spirit of God, rises far above the old Chaldæans and their dreams. Perhaps the captive Jews were tempted to worship these cherubim and genii, as the Chaldæans did; and it may be that Ezekiel was commissioned by God to set them right, and by his vision to give a type, pattern, or picture of God's spiritual laws, by which He rules the world.

Be that as it may. In the first place, Ezekiel's cherubim are far more wonderful and complicated than those which he would see on the walls of the Assyrian buildings. And rightly so; for this world is far more wonderful, more complicated, more cunningly made and ruled, than any of man's fancies about it; as it is written in the Book of Job,—'Where wast thou when I laid the foundations of the earth? declare, if thou hast understanding. Whereupon are the foundations thereof fastened? or who laid the corner-stone thereof; when the morning stars sang together, and all the sons of God shouted for joy?'

Next (and this is most important), these different cherubim were not independent of each other, each going his own way, and doing his own will. Not so Ezekiel had found in them a divine and wonderful order, by which the services of angels as well as of men are constituted. Orderly and harmoniously they worked together. Out of the same fiery globe, from the same throne of God, they came forth all alike. They turned not when they went; whithersoever the Spirit was to go, they went, and ran and returned like a flash of lightning. Nay, in one place he speaks as if all the four creatures were but one creature: 'This is the living creature which I saw by the river of Chebar.'

And so it is, we may be sure, in the world of God, whether in the earthly or in the heavenly world. All things work together, praising God and doing His will. Angels and the heavenly host; sun and moon; stars and light; fire and hail; snow and vapour; wind and storm: all fulfil His word. 'He hath made them fast for ever and ever: He hath given them a law which shall not be broken.' For before all things, under all things, and through all things, is a divine unity and order; all things working towards one end, because all things spring from one beginning, which is the bosom of God the Father.

And so with the wheels; the wheels of fortune and victory, and the fate of nations and of kings. 'They were so high,' Ezekiel said, 'that they were dreadful.' But he saw no human genius sitting, one in each wheel of fortune, each protecting his favourite king and nation. These, too, did not go their own way and of their own will. They were parts of God's divine and wonderful order, and obeyed the same laws as the cherubim. 'And when the living creatures went, the wheels went with them; for the spirit of the living creature was in the wheels.' Everywhere was the same divine unity and order; the same providence, the same laws of God, presided over the natural world and over the fortunes of nations and of kings. Victory and prosperity was not given arbitrarily by separate genii, each genius protecting his favourite king, each genius striving against the other on behalf of his favourite. Fortune came from the providence of One Being; of Him of whom it is written, 'God standeth in the congregation of princes: He is the judge among gods.' And again, 'The Lord is King, be the people never so impatient: He sitteth between the cherubim, be the earth never so unquiet.'

And is this all? God forbid. This is more than the Chaldæans saw, who worshipped angels and not God—the creature instead of the Creator. But where the Chaldæan vision ended, Ezekiel's only began. His prophecy rises far above the imaginations of the heathen.

He hears the sound of the wings of the cherubim, like the tramp of an army, like the noise of great waters, like the roll of thunder, the voice of Almighty God: but above their wings he sees a firmament, which the heathen cannot see, clear as the flashing crystal, and on that firmament a sapphire throne, and round that throne a rainbow, the type of forgiveness and faithfulness, and on that throne A Man.

And the cherubim stand, and let down their wings in submission, waiting for the voice of One mightier than they. And Ezekiel falls upon his face, and hears from off the throne a human voice, which calls to him as human likewise, 'Son of man, stand upon thy feet, and I will speak to thee.'

This, this is Ezekiel's vision: not the fiery globe merely, nor the cherubim, nor the wheels, nor the powers of nature, nor the angelic host—dominions and principalities, and powers—but The Man enthroned above them all, the Lord and Guide and Ruler of the universe; He who makes the winds His angels, and the flames of fire His ministers; and that Lord speaking to him, not through cherubim, not through angels, not through nature, not through mediators, angelic or human, but speaking direct to him himself, as man speaks to man.

As man speaks to man. This is the very pith and marrow of the Old Testament and of the New; which gradually unfolds itself, from the very first chapter of Genesis to the last of Revelation,—that man is made in the likeness of God; and that therefore God can speak to him, and he can understand God's words and inspirations.

Man is like God; and therefore God, in some inconceivable way, is like man. That is the great truth set forth in the first chapter of Genesis, which goes on unfolding itself more clearly throughout the Old Testament, till here, in Ezekiel's vision, it comes to, perhaps, its clearest stage save one.

That human appearance speaks to Ezekiel, the hapless prisoner of war, far away from his native land. And He speaks to him with human voice, and claims kindred with him as a human being, saying, 'Son of man.' That is very deep and wonderful. The Lord upon His throne does not wish Ezekiel to think how different He is to him, but how like He is to him. He says not to Ezekiel,—'Creature infinitely below Me! Dust and ashes, unworthy to appear in My presence! Worm of the earth, as far below Me and unlike Me as the worm under thy feet is to thee!' but, 'Son of man; creature made in My image and likeness, be not afraid! Stand on thy feet, and be a man; and speak to others what I speak to thee.'

After that great revelation of God there seems but one step more to make it perfect; and that step was made in God's good time, in the Incarnation of our Lord Jesus Christ.

Forasmuch as the children are partakers of flesh and blood, He also—He whom Ezekiel saw in human form enthroned on high—He took part of flesh and blood likewise, and was not ashamed, yea, rather rejoiced, to call Himself, what He called Ezekiel, the Son of Man.

'And the Word was made flesh, and dwelt among us; and we beheld His glory.' And why?

For many reasons; but certainly for this one. To make men feel more utterly and fully what Ezekiel was made to feel. That God could thoroughly feel for man; and that man could thoroughly trust God.

That God could thoroughly feel for man. For we have a High Priest who has been made perfect by sufferings, tempted in all points like as we are; and we can

> 'Look to Him who, not in vain,
> Experienced every human pain;
> He sees our wants, allays our fears,
> And counts and treasures up our tears.'

Again,—That man could utterly trust God. For when St. John and his companions (simple fishermen) beheld the glory of Jesus, the Incarnate Word, what was it like? It was 'full of grace and truth;' the perfection of human graciousness, of human truthfulness, which could win and melt the hearts of simple folk, and make them see in Him, who was called the carpenter's son, the beauty of the glory of the Godhead.

'He is the Judge of all the earth.' And why? Let Him Himself tell us. He says that the Father has given the Son authority to execute judgment. And why, once more? Because He is the Son of God? Our Lord says more, 'Because,' He says, 'He is the Son of Man;' who knows what is in man; who can feel, understand, discriminate, pity, make allowances, judge fair, and righteous, and merciful judgment, among creatures whose weakness He has experienced, whose temptations He has felt, whose pains and sorrows He has borne in mortal flesh and blood.

Oh, Gospel and good news for the weak, the sorrowful, the oppressed; for those who are wearied with the burden of their sins, or wearied also by the burden of heavy responsibilities, and awful public duties! When all mortal counsellors fail them, when all mortal help is too weak, let them but throw themselves on the mercy of Him who sits upon the throne, and remember that He, though immortal and eternal, is still the Son of Man, who knows what is in man.

There are times in which we are all tempted to worship other things than God. Not, perhaps, to worship cherubim and genii, angels and spirits, like the old Chaldees, but to worship the laws of political economy, the laws of statesmanship, the powers of nature, the laws of physical science, those lower messengers of God's providence, of which St. Paul says, 'He maketh the winds His angels, and flames of fire His ministers.'

In such times we have need to remember Ezekiel's lesson, that above them all, ruling and guiding, sits He whose form is as the Son of Man.

We are not to say that any powers of nature are evil, or the laws of any science false. Heaven forbid! Ezekiel did not say that the cherubim were evil, or meaningless; or that the belief in angels ministering to man was false. He said the very opposite. But he said, All these obey one whose form is that of a man. He rules them, and they do His will. They are but ministering spirits before Him.

Therefore we are not to disbelieve science, nor disregard the laws of nature, or we shall lose by our folly. But we are to believe that nature and science are not our gods. They do not rule us; our fortunes are not in their hands. Above nature and above science sits the Lord of nature and the Lord of science. Above all the counsels of princes, and the struggles of nations, and the chances and changes of this world of man, sits the Judge of princes and of peoples, the Lord of all the nations upon earth, He by whom all things were made, and who upholdeth all things by the word of His power; and He is man, of the substance of His mother; most human and yet most divine; full of justice and truth, full of care and watchfulness, full of love and pity, full of tenderness and understanding; a Friend, a Guide, a Counsellor, a Comforter, a Saviour to all who trust in Him. He is nearer to us than nature and science: and He should be dearer to us; for they speak only to our understanding; but He speaks to our human hearts, to our inmost spirits. Nature and science cannot take away our sins, give peace to our hearts, right judgment to our minds, strength to our wills, or everlasting life to our souls and bodies. But there sits One upon the throne who can. And if nature were to vanish away, and science were to be proved (however correct as far as it went) a mere child's guess about this wonderful world, which none can understand save He who made it—if all the counsels of princes and of peoples, however just and wise, were to be confounded and come to nought, still, after all, and beyond all, and above all, Christ would abide for ever, with human tenderness yearning over human hearts; with human wisdom teaching human ignorance; with human sympathy sorrowing with human mourners; for ever saying, 'Come unto me, ye that are weary and heavy laden, and I will give you rest.'

Cherubim and seraphim, angels and archangels, dominions and powers, whether of nature or of grace—these all serve Him and do His work. He has constituted their services in a wonderful order: but He has not taken their nature on Him. Our nature He has taken on Him, that we might be bone of His bone and flesh of His flesh; able to say to

Him for ever, in all the chances and changes of this mortal life—

> 'Thou, O Christ, art all I want,
>   More than all in thee I find;
> Raise me, fallen; cheer me, faint;
>   Heal me, sick; and lead me, blind.
> Thou of life the fountain art,
>   Freely let me drink of Thee;
> Spring Thou up within my heart,
>   Rise to all eternity.'

SERMON X.
RUTH.

Ruth ii. 4.

And, behold, Boaz came from Bethlehem, and said unto the reapers, The Lord be with you. And they answered him, The Lord bless thee.

MOST of you know the story of Ruth, from which my text is taken, and you have thought it, no doubt, a pretty story. But did you ever think why it was in the Bible?

Every book in the Bible is meant to teach us, as the Article of our Church says, something necessary to salvation. But what is there necessary to our salvation in the Book of Ruth?

No doubt we learn from it that Ruth was the ancestress of King David; and that she was, therefore, an ancestress of our blessed Lord Jesus Christ: but curious and interesting as that is, we can hardly call that something necessary to salvation. There must be something more in the book. Let us take it simply as it stands, and see if we can find it out.

It begins by telling us how a man of Bethlehem has been driven out of his own country by a famine, he and his wife Naomi and his two sons, and has gone over the border into Moab, among the heathen; how his two sons have married heathen women, and the name of the one was Ruth, and the name of the other Orpah. Then how he dies, and his two sons; and how Naomi, his widow, hears that the Lord had visited His people, in giving them bread; how the people of Judah were prosperous again, and she is there all alone among the heathen; so she sets out to go back to her own people, and her daughters-in-law go with her.

But she persuades them not to go. Why do they not stay in their own land? And they weep over each other; and Orpah kisses her mother-in-law, and goes back; but Ruth cleaves unto her.

Then follows that famous speech of Ruth's, which, for its simple beauty and poetry, has become a proverb, and even a song, among us to this day.

And Ruth said, 'Intreat me not to leave thee, or to return from following after thee: for whither thou goest, I will go; and where thou lodgest, I will lodge: thy people shall be my people, and thy God my God:

'Where thou diest, will I die, and there will I be buried: the Lord do so to me, and more also, if ought but death part thee and me.'

So when she saw that she was steadfastly minded to go to her, she left speaking to her.

And they come to Bethlehem, and all the town was moved about them; and they said, Is this Naomi?

'And she said unto them, Call me not Naomi, call me Mara: for the Almighty hath dealt very bitterly with me. I went out full, and the Lord hath brought me home again empty: why then call ye me Naomi, seeing the Lord hath testified against me, and the Almighty hath afflicted me?'

And they came to Bethlehem about the passover tide, at the beginning of barley harvest, and Ruth went out into the fields to glean, and she lighted on a part of the field which belonged to Boaz, who was of her husband's kindred.

And Boaz was a mighty man of wealth, according to the simple fashions of that old land and old time. Not like one of our great modern noblemen, or merchants, but rather like one of our wealthy yeomen: a man who would not disdain to work in his field with his own slaves, after the wholesome fashion of those old times, when a royal prince and mighty warrior would sow the corn with his own hands, while his man opened the furrow with the plough before him. There Boaz dwelt, with other yeomen, up among the limestone hills, in the little walled village of Bethlehem, which was afterwards to become so famous and so holy; and had, we may suppose, his vineyard and his olive-garden on the rocky slopes, and his corn-fields in the vale below, and his flock of sheep and goats feeding on the downs; while all his wealth besides lay, probably, after the Eastern fashion, in one great chest—full of rich dresses, and gold and silver ornaments, and coins, all foreign, got in exchange for his corn, and wine, and oil, from Assyrian, or Egyptian, or Phœnician traders; for the Jews then had no money, and very little manufacture, of their own.

And he would have had hired servants, too, and slaves, in his house; treated kindly enough, as members of the family, eating and drinking at his table, and faring nearly as well as he fared himself.

A stately, God-fearing man he plainly was; respectable, courteous, and upright, and altogether worthy of his wealth; and he went out into the field, looking after his reapers in the barley harvest—about our Easter-tide.

And he said to his reapers, The Lord be with you. And they answered, The Lord bless thee.

Then he saw Ruth, who had happened to light upon his field, gleaning after the reapers, and found out who she was, and bid her glean without fear, and abide by his maidens, for he had charged the young men that they shall not touch her.

'And Boaz said unto her, At meal-time come thou

hither, and eat of the bread, and dip thy morsel in the vinegar. And she sat beside the reapers: and he reached her parched corn, and she did eat, and was sufficed, and left.

'And when she was risen up to glean, Boaz commanded his young men, saying, Let her glean even among the sheaves, and reproach her not: and let fall also some of the handfuls of purpose for her, and leave them, that she may glean them, and rebuke her not.

'So she gleaned in the field until even, and beat out that she had gleaned: and it was about an ephah of barley.'

Then follows the simple story, after the simple fashion of those days. How Naomi bids Ruth wash and anoint herself, and put on her best garments, and go down to Boaz' floor (his barn as we should call it now) where he is going to eat, and drink, and sleep, and there claim his protection as a near kinsman.

And how Ruth comes in softly and lies down at his feet, and how he treats her honourably and courteously, and promises to protect her. But there is a nearer kinsman than he, and he must be asked first if he will do the kinsman's part, and buy his cousin's plot of land, and marry his cousin's widow with it.

And how Boaz goes to the town-gate next day, and sits down in the gate (for the porch of the gate was a sort of town-hall or vestry-room in the East, wherein all sorts of business was done), and there he challenges the kinsman,—Will he buy the ground and marry Ruth? And he will not: he cannot afford it. Then Boaz calls all the town to witness that day, that he has bought all that was Elimelech's, and Ruth the Moabitess to be his wife.

'And all the people that were in the gate, and the elders, said, We are witnesses. The Lord make the woman that is come into thine house like Rachel and like Leah, which two did build the house of Israel: and do thou worthily in Ephratah, and be famous in Bethlehem.'

And in due time Ruth had a son. 'And the women said unto Naomi, Blessed be the Lord, which hath not left thee this day without a kinsman, that his name may be famous in Israel.

'And he shall be unto thee a restorer of thy life, and a nourisher of thine old age: for thy daughter-in-law, which loveth thee, which is better to thee than seven sons, hath born him.

'And Naomi took the child, and laid it in her bosom, and became nurse unto it.

'And the women her neighbours gave it a name, saying, There is a son born to Naomi; and they called his name Obed: he is the father of Jesse, the father of David.'

And so ends the Book of Ruth.

Now, my friends, can you not answer for yourselves the question which I asked at first,—Why is the story of Ruth in the Bible, and what may we learn from it which is necessary for our salvation?

I think, at least, that you will be able to answer it—if not in words, still in your hearts—if you will read the book for yourselves.

For does it not consecrate to God that simple country life which we lead here? Does it not tell us that it is blessed in the sight of Him who makes the grass to grow, and the corn to ripen in its season?

Does it not tell us, that not only on the city and the palace, on the cathedral and the college, on the assemblies of statesmen, on the studies of scholars, but upon the meadow and the corn-field, the farm-house and the cottage, is written, by the everlasting finger of God—Holiness unto the Lord? That it is all blessed in His sight; that the simple dwellers in villages, the simple tillers of the ground, can be as godly and as pious, as virtuous and as high-minded, as those who have nought to do but to serve God in the offices of religion? Is it not an honour and a comfort, to such as us, to find one whole book of the Holy Bible occupied by the simplest story of the fortunes of a yeoman's family, in a lonely village among the hills of Judah? True, the yeoman's widow became the ancestress of David, and of his mighty line of kings—nay, the ancestress of our Lord Jesus Christ Himself. But the Book of Ruth was not written mainly to tell us that fact. It mentions it at the end, and as it were by accident. The book itself is taken up with the most simple and careful details of country life, country customs, country folk—as if that was what we were to think of, as we read of Ruth. And that is what we do think of—not of the ancestress of kings, but of the fair young heathen gleaning among the corn, with the pious, courteous, high-minded yeoman bidding her abide fast by his maidens, and when she was athirst drink of the wine which the young men have drawn, for it has been fully showed him all she has done for her mother-in-law; and the Lord will recompense her work, and a full reward be given her of the Lord God of Israel, under the shadow of whose wings she is to come to trust. That is the scene which painters naturally draw; that is what we naturally think of; because God, who gave us the Bible, meant us to think thereof; and to know, that working in the quiet village, or in the distant field, women may be as pure and modest, men as high-minded and well-bred, and both as full of the fear of God, and the thought that God's eye is upon them, as if they were in a place, or a station, where they had nothing to do but to watch over the salvation of their own souls; that the meadow and the harvest-field need not .be, as they too often are, places for temptation and for defilement; where the old too often teach the young, not to fear God and keep themselves pure, but to copy their coarse jests and foul language, and listen to stories which had better be buried for ever in the dirt out of which they spring. You know what I mean. You know what field-work too often is. Read the Book of Ruth, and see what field-work may be, and ought to be.

Yes, my dear friends. Pure you may be, and gentle, upright, and godly, about your daily work, if the Spirit of God be within you.

Country life has its temptations: and so has town life, and every life. But there has no temptation taken you save such as is common to man. Boaz, the rich yeoman; Naomi, the broken-hearted and ruined; Ruth, the fair young widow—all had the very same temptations as are common to you now, here; but they conquered them, because they feared God and kept His commandments; and to know that, is necessary for your salvation.

And, looked at in this light, the Book of Ruth is indeed a prophecy; a forecast and a shadow of the teaching of the Lord Jesus Himself, who spake to country folk as never man spake before, and bade them look upon the simple, every-day matters which were around them in field and wood, and open their eyes to the Divine lessons of God's providence, which also were all around them; who, born Himself in that little village of

Bethlehem, and brought up in the little village of Nazareth, among the lonely lanes and downs, spoke of country things to country folk, and bade them read in the great green book which God has laid open before them all day long. Who bade them to consider the lilies of the field, how they grew, and the ravens, how God fed them; to look on the fields, white for harvest, and pray God to send labourers into his spiritual harvest-field; to look on the tares which grew among the wheat, and know we must not try to part them ourselves, but leave that to God at the last day; to look on the fishers, who were casting their net into the Lake of Galilee, and sorting the fish upon the shore, and be sure that a day was coming, when God would separate the good from the bad, and judge every man according to his work and worth; and to learn from the common things of country life the rule of the living God, and the laws of the kingdom of heaven.

One word more, and I have done.

The story of Ruth is also the consecration of woman's love. I do not mean of the love of wife to husband, divine and blessed as that is. I mean that depth and strength of devotion, tenderness, and self-sacrifice, which God has put in the heart of all true women; and which they spend so strangely, and so nobly often, on persons who have no claim on them, from whom they can receive no earthly reward;—the affection which made women minister of their substance to our Lord Jesus Christ; which brought Mary Magdalene to the foot of the Cross, and to the door of the tomb, that she might at least see the last of Him whom she thought lost to her for ever; the affection which has made a wise man say, that as long as women and sorrow are left in the world, so long will the Gospel of our Lord Jesus live and conquer therein; the affection which makes women round us every day ministering angels, wherever help or comfort are needed; which makes many a woman do deeds of unselfish goodness known only to God; not known even to herself; for she does them by instinct, by the inspiration of God's Spirit, without self-consciousness or pride, without knowing what noble things she is doing, without spoiling the beauty of her good work by even admitting to herself, 'What a good work it is! How right she is in doing it! How much it will advance the salvation of her own soul!'—but thinking herself, perhaps, a very useless and paltry person; while the angels of God are claiming her as their sister and their peer.

Yes, if there is a woman in this congregation—and there is one, I will warrant, in every congregation in England—who is devoting herself for the good of others; giving up the joys of life to take care of orphans who have no legal claim on her; or to nurse a relation, who perhaps repays her with little but exacting peevishness; or who has spent all her savings, in bringing up her brothers, or in supporting her parents in their old age,— then let her read the story of Ruth, and be sure that, like Ruth, she will be repaid by the Lord. Her reward may not be the same as Ruth's: but it will be that which is best for her, and she shall in no wise lose her reward. If she has given up all for Christ, it shall be repaid her ten-fold in this life, and in the world to come life everlasting. If, with Ruth, she is true to the inspirations of God's Spirit, then, with Ruth, God will be true to her. Let her endure, for in due time she shall reap, if she faint not;—and to know that, is necessary for her salvation.

SERMON XI.

SOLOMON.

ECCLESIASTES i. 12—14.

I the Preacher was king over Israel in Jerusalem. And I gave my heart to seek and search out by wisdom concerning all things that are done under heaven: this sore travail hath God given to the sons of man to be exercised therewith. I have seen all the works that are done under the sun; and, behold, all is vanity and vexation of spirit.

ALL have heard of Solomon the Wise. His name has become a proverb among men. It was still more a proverb among the old Rabbis, the lawyers and scribes of the Gospels.

Their hero, the man of whom they delighted to talk and dream, was not David, the Psalmist, and the shepherd-boy, the man of many wanderings, and many sorrows: but his son Solomon, with all his wealth, and pomp and magic wisdom. Ever since our Lord's time, if not before it, Solomon has been the national hero of the Jews; while David, as the truer type and pattern of the Lord Jesus Christ, has been the hero of Christians.

The Rabbis, with their Eastern fancy—childishly fond, to this day, of gold, and jewels, and outward pomp and show—would talk and dream of the lost glories of Solomon's court; of his gilded and jewelled temple, with its pillars of sandal-wood from Ophir, and its sea of molten brass; of his ivory lion-throne, and his three hundred golden shields; of his fleets which went away into the far Indian sea, and came back after three years with foreign riches and curious beasts. And as if that had not been enough, they delighted to add to the truth fable upon fable. The Jews, after the time of the Babylonish captivity, seem to have more and more identified Wisdom with mere Magic; and therefore Solomon was, in their eyes, the master of all magicians. He knew the secrets of the stars, and of the elements, the secrets of all charms and spells. By virtue of his magic seal he had power over all those evil spirits, with which the Jews believed the earth and sky to be filled. He could command all spirits, force them to appear to him and bow before him, and send them to the ends of the earth to do his bidding. Nothing so fantastic, nothing so impossible, but those old Scribes and Pharisees imputed it to their idol, Solomon the Wise.

The Bible, of course, has no such fancies in it, and gives us a sober and rational account of Solomon's wisdom, and of Solomon's greatness.

It tells us how, when he was yet young, God appeared

to him in a dream, and said, Ask what I shall give thee. And Solomon made answer—

'.... O Lord my God, Thou hast made Thy servant king instead of David my father; and I am but a little child: I know not how to go out or come in.

'Give therefore Thy servant an understanding heart to judge Thy people, that I may discern between good and bad: for who is able to judge this Thy so great a people?

'And the speech pleased the Lord, that Solomon had asked this thing.

'And God said unto him, Because thou hast asked this thing, and hast not asked for thyself long life; neither hast asked riches for thyself, nor hast asked the life of thine enemies; but hast asked for thyself understanding to discern judgment:

'Behold, I have done according to thy words: lo, I have given thee a wise and an understanding heart; so that there was none like thee before thee, neither after thee shall any arise like unto thee.

'And I have also given thee that which thou hast not asked, both riches and honour: so that there shall not be any among the kings like unto thee all thy days.'

And the promise, says Solomon himself, was fulfilled.

In his days Judah and Israel were many, as the sand which is by the sea-shore, for multitude, eating and drinking and making merry; and Solomon reigned over all kings, from the river to the land of the Philistines and the border of Egypt; and they brought presents, and served Solomon all the days of his life. And he had peace on all sides round about him. And Judah and Israel dwelt safely, every man under his own vine and his own fig-tree, all the days of Solomon.

'I was great,' he says, 'and increased more than all that were before me in Jerusalem; also my wisdom remained with me. And whatsoever mine eyes desired I kept not from them; I withheld not my heart from any joy; for my heart rejoiced in all my labour....

'Then I looked on all the works that my hands had wrought, and on the labour that I had laboured to do: and, behold, all was vanity and vexation of spirit, and there was no profit under the sun.

'And I turned myself to behold wisdom, and madness, and folly: for what can the man do that cometh after the king? even that which hath been already done.'

Yes, my dear friends, we are too apt to think of exceeding riches, or wisdom, or power, or glory, as unalloyed blessings from God. How many are there who would say,—if it were not happily impossible for them,—Oh that I were like Solomon! Happy man that he was, to be able to say of himself, 'I was great, and increased more than all that were before me in

Jerusalem. And whatsoever mine eyes desired, I kept not from them; I withheld not my heart from any joy, for my heart rejoiced in all my labour.'

To have everything that he wanted, to be able to do anything that he liked—was he not a happy man? Is not such a life a Paradise on earth?

Yes, my friends, it is. But it is the Paradise of fools.

Yet, Solomon was not a fool. He says expressly that his wisdom remained with him through all his labour. Through all his pleasure he kept alive the longing after knowledge. He even tried, as he says, wine, and mirth, and folly, yet acquainting himself with wisdom. He would try that, as well as statesmanship, and the rule of a great kingdom, and the building of temples and palaces, and the planting of parks and gardens, and his three thousand Proverbs, and his Songs a thousand and five; and his speech of beasts and of birds and of all plants, from the cedar in Lebanon to the hyssop which groweth on the wall. He would know everything, and try everything. If he was luxurious and proud, he would be no idler, no useless gay liver. He would work, and discern, and know,—and at last he found it all out, and this was the sum thereof—

'Vanity of vanities, saith the Preacher; all is vanity.'

He found no rest in pleasure, riches, power, glory, wisdom itself; he had learnt nothing more after all than he might have known, and doubtless did know, when he was a child of seven years old. And that was, simply to fear God and keep His commandments; for that was the whole duty of man.

But though he knew it, he had lost the power of doing it; and he ended darkly and shamefully, a dotard worshipping idols of wood and stone, among his heathen queens. And thus, as in David the height of chivalry fell to the deepest baseness; so in Solomon the height of wisdom fell to the deepest folly.

My friends, the truth is, that exceeding gifts from God like Solomon's are not blessings, they are duties; and very solemn and heavy duties. They do not increase a man's happiness; they only increase his responsibility—the awful account which he must give at last of the talents committed to his charge. They increase, too, his danger. They increase the chance of his having his head turned to pride and pleasure, and falling shamefully, and coming to a miserable end. As with David, so with Solomon. Man is nothing, and God is all in all.

And as with David and Solomon, so with many a king and many a great man. Consider those who have been great and glorious in their day. And in how many cases they have ended sadly! The burden of glory has been too heavy for them to bear; they have broken down under it.

The great Charles the Fifth, Emperor of Germany and King of Spain and all the Indies: our own great Queen Elizabeth, who found England all but ruined, and left her strong and rich, glorious and terrible: Lord Bacon, the wisest of all mortal men since the time of Solomon: and, in our own fathers' time, Napoleon Buonaparte, the poor young officer, who rose to be the conqueror of half Europe, and literally the king of kings,—how have they all ended? In sadness and darkness, vanity and vexation of spirit.

Oh, my friends! if ever proud and ambitious thoughts arise in any of our hearts, let us crush them down till we can say with David: 'Lord, my heart is not haughty, nor mine eyes lofty; neither do I exercise myself in great matters, or in things too high for me.

'Surely I have behaved and quieted myself, as a child that is weaned of his mother; my soul is even as a weaned child.'

And if ever idle and luxurious thoughts arise in our hearts, and we are tempted to say, 'Soul, thou hast much goods laid up for many years; take thine ease, eat, drink, and be merry;' let us hear the word of the Lord crying against us: 'Thou fool! This night shall thy soul be required of thee. Then whose shall those things be which thou hast provided?'

Let us pray, my friends, for that great—I had almost said, that crowning grace and virtue of moderation, what

St. Paul calls sobriety and a sound mind. Let us pray for moderate appetites, moderate passions, moderate honours, moderate gains, moderate joys; and, if sorrows be needed to chasten us, moderate sorrows. Let us long violently after nothing, or wish too eagerly to rise in life; and be sure that what the Apostle says of those who long to be rich is equally true of those who long to be famous, or powerful, or in any way to rise over the heads of their fellow-men. They all fall, as the Apostle says, into foolish and hurtful lusts, which drown men in destruction and perdition, and so pierce themselves through with many sorrows.

And let us thank God heartily if He has put us into circumstances which do not tempt us to wild and vain hopes of becoming rich, or great or admired by men.

Especially let us thank Him for this quiet country life which we lead here, free from ambition, and rash speculation, and the hope of great and sudden gains. All know, who have watched the world, how unwholesome for a man's soul any trade or occupation is which offers the chance of making a rapid fortune. It has hurt the souls of too many merchants and manufacturers ere now. Good and sober-minded men there are among them, thank God, who can resist the temptation, and are content to go along the plain path of quiet and patient honesty; but to those who have not the sober spirit, who have not the fear of God before their eyes the temptation is too terrible to withstand; and it is not withstood; and therefore the columns of our newspapers are so often filled with sad cases of bankruptcy, forgery, extravagant and desperate trading, bubble fortunes spent in a few years of vain show and luxury, and ending in poverty and shame.

Happy, on the other hand, are those who till the ground; who never can rise high enough, or suddenly enough, to turn their heads; whose gains are never great and quick enough to tempt them to wild speculation: but who can, if they will only do their duty patiently and well, go on year after year in quiet prosperity, and be content to offer up, week by week, Agur's wise prayer: 'Give me neither poverty nor riches, but feed me with food sufficient for me.'

They need never complain that they have no time to think of their own souls; that the hurry and bustle of business must needs drive religion out of their minds. Their life passes in a quiet round of labours. Day after day, week after week, season after season, they know beforehand what they have to do, and can arrange their affairs for this world, so as to give them full time to think of the world to come. Every week brings small gains, for which they can thank the God of all plenty; and every week brings, too, small anxieties, for which they can trust the same God who has given them His only-begotten Son, and will with Him freely give them all things needful for them; who has, in mercy to their souls and bodies, put them in the healthiest and usefullest of all pursuits, the one which ought to lead their minds most to God, and the one in which (if they be thoughtful men) they have the deep satisfaction of feeling that they are not working for themselves only, but for their fellow-men; that every sheaf of corn they grow is a blessing, not merely to themselves, but to the whole nation.

My friends, think of these things, especially at this rich and blessed harvest-time; and while you thank your God and your Saviour for His unexampled bounty in this year's good harvest, do not forget to thank Him for having given the sowing and the reaping of those crops to you; and for having called you to that business in life in which, I verily believe, you will find it most easy to serve and obey Him, and be least tempted to ambition and speculation, and the lust of riches, and the pride which goes before a fall.

Think of these things; and think of the exceeding mercies which God heaps on you as Englishmen,—peace and safety, freedom and just laws, the knowledge of His Bible, the teaching of His Church, and all that man needs for body and soul. Let those who have thanked God already, thank Him still more earnestly, and show their thankfulness not only in their lips, but in their lives; and let those who have not thanked Him, awake, and learn, as St. Paul bids them, from God's own witness of Himself, in that He has sent them fruitful seasons, filling their hearts with food and gladness:—let them learn, I say, from that, that they have a Father in heaven who has given them His only-begotten Son, and will with Him freely give them all things needful: only asking in return that they should obey His laws—to obey which is everlasting life.

SERMON XII.

PROGRESS.

(Preached before the Queen at Clifden, June 3, 1866.)

ECCLESIASTES vii. 10.

Say not thou, What is the cause that the former days were better than these? for thou dost not inquire wisely concerning this.

THIS text occurs in the Book of Ecclesiastes, which has been for many centuries generally attributed to Solomon the son of David. I say generally, because, not only among later critics, but even among the ancient Jewish Rabbis, there have been those who doubted or denied that Solomon was its author.

I cannot presume to decide on such a question: but it seems to me most probable, that the old tradition is right, even though the book may have suffered alterations, both in form and in language: but any later author, personating Solomon, would surely have put into his mouth very different words from those of Ecclesiastes. Solomon was the ideal hero-king of the later Jews. Stories of his superhuman wealth, of magical power, of a fabulous extent of dominion, grew up about his name. He who was said to control, by means of his wondrous seal, the genii of earth and air, would scarcely have been represented as a disappointed and broken-hearted sage, who pronounced all human labour to be vanity and vexation of spirit; who saw but one event for the righteous and the wicked, and the wise man and the fool; and questioned bitterly whether there was any future state, any pre-eminence in man over the brute.

These, and other startling utterances, made certain of the early Rabbis doubt the authenticity and inspiration of the Book of Ecclesiastes, as containing things contrary to the Law, and to desire its suppression, till they discovered in it—as we may, if we be wise—a weighty and world-wide meaning.

Be that as it may, it would certainly be a loss to Scripture, and to our knowledge of humanity, if it was proved that this book, in its original shape, was not written by a great king, and most probably by Solomon himself. The book gains by that fact, not only in its reality and truthfulness, but in its value and importance as a lesson of human life. Especially does this text gain; for it has a natural and deep connection with Solomon and his times.

The former days were better than his days: he could not help seeing that they were. He must have feared lest the generation which was springing up should inquire into the reason thereof, in a tone which would breed—which actually did breed—discontent and revolution.

But the fact seemed at first sight patent. The old heroic days of Samuel and David were past. The Jewish race no longer produced such men as Saul and Jonathan, as Joab and Abner. A generation of great men, whose names are immortal, had died out, and a generation of inferior men, of whom hardly one name has come down to us, had succeeded them. The nation had lost its primæval freedom, and the courage and loyalty which freedom gives. It had become rich, and enervated by luxury and ease. Solomon had civilised the Jewish kingdom, till it had become one of the greatest nations of the East; but it had become also, like the other nations of the East, a vast and gaudy despotism, hollow and rotten to the core; ready to fall to pieces at Solomon's death, by selfishness, disloyalty, and civil war. Therefore it was that Solomon hated all his labour that he had wrought under the sun; for all was vanity and vexation of spirit.

Such were the facts. And yet it was not wise to look at them too closely; not wise to inquire why the former times were better than those. So it was. Let it alone. Pry not too curiously into the past, or into the future; but do the duty which lies nearest to thee. Fear God and keep His commandments. For that is the whole duty of man.

Thus does Solomon lament over the certain decay of the Jewish Empire. And his words, however sad, are indeed eternal and inspired. For they have proved true, and will prove true to the end, of every despotism of the East, or empire formed on Eastern principles; of the old Persian Empire, of the Roman, of the Byzantine, of those of Hairoun Alraschid and of Aurungzebe, of those Turkish and Chinese-Tartar empires whose dominion is decaying before our very eyes. Of all these the wise man's words are true. They are vanity and vexation of spirit. That which is crooked cannot be made straight, and that which is wanting cannot be numbered. The thing which has been is that which shall be, and there is no new thing under the sun. Incapacity of progress; the same outward civilization repeating itself again and again; the same intrinsic certainty of decay and death;—these are the marks of all empire, which is not founded on that foundation which is laid, even Jesus Christ.

But of Christian nations these words are not true. They pronounce the doom of the old world: but the new world has no part in them, unless it copies the sins and follies of the old.

It is not true of Christian nations that the thing which has been is that which shall be; and that there is no new thing under the sun. For over them is the kingdom of Christ, the Saviour of all men, specially of them which believe, the King of all the princes of the earth, who has always asserted, and will for ever assert, His own overruling dominion. And in them is the Spirit of God, which is the spirit of truth and righteousness; of improvement, discovery, progress from darkness to light, from folly to wisdom, from barbarism to justice, and mercy, and the true civilization of the heart and spirit.

And, therefore, for us it is not only an act of prudence, but a duty; a duty of faith in God; a duty of loyalty to Jesus Christ our Lord, not to ask, Why the former times were better than these? For they were not better than these. Every age has had its own special nobleness, its own special use : but every age has been better than the age which went before it; for the Spirit of God is leading the ages on, toward that whereof it is written, 'Eye hath not seen nor ear heard, nor hath it entered into the heart of man to conceive, the things which God hath prepared for those that love Him.'

Very unfaithful are we to the teaching of God's Spirit; many and heavy are our sins against light and knowledge, and means, and opportunities of grace. But let us not add to those sins the sin (for such it is) of inquiring why the former times were better than these.

For, first, the inquiry shows disbelief in our Lord's own words, that all dominion is given to Him in heaven and earth, and that He is with us always, even to the end of the world. And next, it is a vain inquiry, based on a mistake. When we look back longingly to any past age, we look not at the reality, but at a sentimental and untrue picture of our own imagination. When we look back longingly to the so-called ages of faith, to the personal loyalty of the old Cavaliers; when we regret that there are no more among us such giants in statesmanship and power as those who brought Europe through the French Revolution; when we long that our lot was cast in any age beside our own, we know not what we ask. The ages which seem so beautiful afar off, would look to us, were we in them, uglier than our own. If we long to be back in those so-called devout ages of faith, we long for an age in which witches and heretics were burned alive; if we long after the chivalrous loyalty of the old Cavaliers, we long for an age in which stage-plays were represented, even before a virtuous monarch like Charles I., which the lowest of our playgoers would not now tolerate. When we long for anything that is past, we long, it may be, for a little good which we seem to have lost; but we long also for real and fearful evil, which, thanks be to God, we have lost likewise. We are not, indeed, to fancy this age perfect, and boast, like some, of the glorious nineteenth century. We are to keep our eyes open to all its sins and defects, that we may amend them. And we are to remember, in fear and trembling, that to us much is given, and of us much is required. But we are to thank God that our lot is cast in an age which, on the whole, is better than any age whatsoever that has gone before it, and to do our best that the age which is coming may be better even than this.

We are neither to regret the past, nor rest satisfied in the present; but, like St. Paul, forgetting those things that are behind us, and reaching onward to those things that are before us, press forward, each and all, to the prize of our high calling in Jesus Christ.

And as with nations and empires, so with our own private lives. It is not wise to ask why the former times were better than these. It is natural, pardonable: but not wise; because we are so apt to mistake the subject about which we ask, and when we say, 'Why were the old times better?' merely to mean, 'Why were the old times happier?' That is not the question. There is something higher than happiness, says a wise man. There is blessedness; the blessedness of being good and doing good, of being right and doing right. That blessedness we may have at all times; we may be blest even in anxiety and in sadness; we may be blest, even as the martyrs of old were blest—in agony and death.

The times are to us whatsoever our character makes them. And if we are better men than we were in former times, then is the present better than the past, even though it be less happy. And why should it not be better? Surely the Spirit of God, the spirit of progress and improvement, is working in us, the children of God, as well as in the great world around. Surely the years ought to have made us better, more useful, more worthy. We may have been disappointed in our lofty ideas of what ought to be done. But we may have gained more clear and practical notions of what can be done. We may have lost in enthusiasm, and yet gained in earnestness. We may have lost in sensibility, yet gained in charity, activity, and power. We may be able to do far less, and yet what we do may be far better done.

And our very griefs and disappointments — Have they been useless to us? Surely not. We shall have gained, instead of lost, by them, if the Spirit of God be working in us. Our sorrows will have wrought in us patience, our patience experience of God's sustaining grace, who promises that as our day our strength shall be; and of God's tender providence, which tempers the wind to the shorn lamb, and lays on none a burden beyond what they are able to bear. And that experience will have worked in us hope: hope that He who has led us thus far will lead us farther still; that He who brought us through the trials of youth, will bring us through the trials of age; that He who taught us in former days precious lessons, not only by sore temptations, but most sacred joys, will teach us in the days to come fresh lessons by temptations which we shall be more able to endure; and by joys which, though unlike those of old times, are no less sacred, no less sent as lessons to our souls, by Him from whom all good gifts come.

We will believe this. And instead of inquiring why the former days were better than these, we will trust that the coming days shall be better than these, and those which are coming after them better still again, because God is our Father, Christ our Saviour, the Holy Ghost our Comforter and Guide. We will toil onward: because we know we are toiling upward. We will live in hope, not in regret; because hope is the only state of mind fit for a race for whom God has condescended to stoop, and suffer, and die, and rise again. We will believe that we, and all we love, whether in earth or heaven, are destined—if we be only true to God's Spirit—to rise, improve, progress for ever: and so we will claim our share, and keep our place, in that vast ascending and improving scale of being, which, as some dream—and surely not in vain—goes onward and upward for ever throughout the universe of Him who wills that none should perish.

SERMON XIII.

FAITH.

(Preached before the Queen at Windsor, December 5, 1865.)

HABAKKUK ii. 4.

The just shall live by his faith.

WE shall always find it most safe, as well as most reverent, to inquire first the literal and exact meaning of a text; to see under what circumstances it was written; what meaning it must have conveyed to those who heard it; and so to judge what it must have meant in the mind of him who spoke it. If we do so, we shall find that the simplest interpretation of Scripture is generally the deepest; and the most literal interpretation is also the most spiritual.

Let us examine the circumstances under which the prophet spake these words.

It was on the eve of a Chaldean invasion. The heathen were coming into Judea, as we see them still in the Assyrian sculptures—civilizing, after their barbarous fashion, the nations round them—conquering, massacring, transporting whole populations, building cities and temples by their forced labour; and resistance or escape was impossible.

The prophet's faith fails him a moment. What is this but a triumph of evil? Is there a Divine Providence? Is there a just Ruler of the world? And he breaks out into pathetic expostulation with God Himself: 'Wherefore lookest Thou upon them that deal treacherously, and holdest Thy tongue when the wicked devoureth the man that is more righteous than he? And makest men as the fishes of the sea, as the creeping things, which have no ruler over them? They take up all of them with the line, they gather them with the net. Therefore they sacrifice unto their net, and burn incense to their line; for by it their portion is fat, and their meat plenteous. Shall they therefore empty their net, and not spare to slay continually the nations?'

Then the Lord answers his doubts: 'Behold, his soul which is lifted up is not upright in him: but the just shall live by his faith.'

By his faith, plainly, in a just Ruler of the world,—in a God who avenges wrong, and makes inquisition for innocent blood. He who will keep his faith in that just God, will remain just himself. The sense of Justice will be kept alive in him; and the just will live by his Faith.

The prophet believes that message; and a mighty

change passes over his spirit. In a burst of magnificent poetry, he proclaims woe to the unjust Chaldean conqueror. All his greatness is a bubble which will burst; a suicidal mistake, which will work out its own punishment, and make him a taunt and a mockery to all nations round. 'Woe to him who increaseth that which is not his, and ladeth himself with thick clay! Woe to him that coveteth an evil covetousness to his house, that he may set his nest on high, and be delivered from the power of evil! Woe to him that buildeth a town with blood, and stablisheth a city with iniquity! Behold, is it not of the Lord of hosts that the people shall labour in the very fire, and the people shall weary themselves for very vanity?' There is a true civilization for man; but not according to the unjust and cruel method of those Chaldeans. The Law of the true Civilization, the prophet says, is this: 'The earth shall be full of the knowledge of the Lord, as the waters cover the sea.'

But what is this to us? Are we like the Chaldeans? God forbid. But are we not tried by the same temptations to which they blindly yielded? A nation, strong, rich, luxurious, prosperous in industry at home, and aggressive (if not in theory, certainly in practice) to less civilized races abroad—are we not tempted daily to that habit of mind which the prophet calls—with that tremendous irony in which the Hebrew prophets surpass

K

all writers—looking on men as the fishes of the sea, as the creeping things which have no ruler over them, born to devour each other, and be caught and devoured in their turn, by a race more cunning than themselves? There are those among us in thousands, thank God, who nobly resist that temptation; and they are the very salt of the land, who keep it from decay. But for the many—for the public—do not too many of them believe that the law of human society is, after all, only that internecine conflict of interests, that brute struggle for existence, which naturalists tell us (and truly) is the law of life for mere plants and animals? Are they not tempted to forget that men are not mere animals and things, but persons; that they have a Ruler over them, even God, who desires to educate them, to sanctify them, to develop their every faculty, that they may be His children, and not merely our tools; and do God's work in the world, and not merely their employer's work? Are they not—are we not all—tempted too often to forget this?

And, then, are we not tempted, all of us, to fall down like the Chaldeans and worship our own net, because by it our portion is fat, and our meat plenteous? Are we not tempted to say within ourselves, 'This present system of things, with all its anomalies and its defects, still is the right system, and the only system. It is the path pointed out by Providence for man. It is of the Lord; for we are comfortable under it. We grow rich under it; we keep rank and power under it: it suits us, pays us. What better proof that it is the perfect system of things, which cannot be amended?'

Meanwhile, we are sorry (for the English are a kind-hearted people) for the victims of our luxury and our neglect. Sorry for the thousands whom we let die every year by preventible diseases, because we are either too busy or too comfortable to save their lives. Sorry for the savages whom we exterminate, by no deliberate evil intent, but by the mere weight of our heavy footstep. Sorry for the thousands who are used-up yearly in certain trades, in ministering to our comfort, even to our very luxuries and frivolities. Sorry for the Sheffield grinders, who go to work as to certain death; who count how many years they have left, and say, 'A short life and a merry one. Let us eat and drink, for tomorrow we die.' Sorry for the people whose lower jaws decay away in lucifer-match factories. Sorry for all the miseries and wrongs which this Children's Employment Commission has revealed. Sorry for the diseases of artificial flower-makers. Sorry for the boys working in glass-houses whole days and nights on end without rest, 'labouring in the very fire, and wearying themselves with very vanity.'—Vanity, indeed, if after an amount of gallant toil which nothing but the indomitable courage of an Englishman could endure, they grow up animals and heathens. We are sorry for them all—as the giant is for the worm on which he treads. Alas! poor worm. But the giant must walk on. He is necessary to the universe, and the worm is not. So we are sorry—for half an hour; and glad too (for we are a kind-hearted people) to hear that charitable persons or the government are going to do something towards alleviating these miseries. And then we return, too many of us, each to his own ambition, or to his own luxury, comforting ourselves with the thought, that we did not make the world, and we are not responsible for it.

How shall we conquer this temptation to laziness, selfishness, heartlessness? By faith in God, such as the prophet had. By faith in God as the eternal enemy of evil, the eternal helper of those who try to overcome evil with good; the eternal avenger of all the wrong which is done on earth. By faith in God, as not only our Father, our Saviour, our Redeemer, our Protector: but the Father, Saviour, Redeemer, Protector, and if need be, Avenger, of every human being. By faith in God, which believes that His infinite heart yearns over every human soul, even the basest and the worst; that He wills that not one little one should perish, but that all should be saved, and come to the knowledge of the truth.

We must believe that, if we wish that it should be

true of us, that the just shall live by his faith. If we wish our faith to keep us just men, leading just lives, we must believe that God is just, and that He shows His justice by the only possible method—by doing justice, sooner or later, for all who are unjustly used.

If we lose that faith, we shall be in danger—in more than danger—of becoming unjust ourselves. As we fancy God to be, so shall we become ourselves. If we believe that God cares little for mankind, we shall care less and less for them ourselves. If we believe that God neglects them, we shall neglect them likewise.

And then the sense of justice—justice for its own sake, justice as the likeness and will of God—will die out in us, and our souls will surely not live, but die.

For there will die out in our hearts, just the most noble and God-like feelings which God has put into them. The instinct of chivalry; horror of cruelty and injustice; pity for the weak and ill-used; the longing to set right whatever is wrong; and, what is even more important, the Spirit of godly fear, of wholesome terror of God's wrath, which makes us say, when we hear of any great and general sin among us, 'If we do not do our best to set this right, then God, who does not make men like creeping things, will take the matter into His own hands, and punish us easy, luxurious people, for allowing such things to be done.'

And when a man loses that spirit of chivalry, he loses his own soul. For that spirit of chivalry, let worldlings say what they will, is the very spirit of our spirit, the salt which keeps our characters from utter decay—the very instinct which raises us above the selfishness of the brute. Yea, it is the Spirit of God Himself. For what is the feeling of horror at wrong, of pity for the wronged, of burning desire to set wrong right, save the Spirit of the Father and the Son, the Spirit which brought down the Lord Jesus out of the highest heaven, to stoop, to serve, to suffer and to die, that He might seek and save that which was lost?

Some say that the age of chivalry is past: that the spirit of romance is dead. The age of chivalry is never past, as long as there is a wrong left unredressed on earth, and a man or woman left to say, 'I will redress that wrong, or spend my life in the attempt.'

The age of chivalry is never past, as long as men have faith enough in God to say, 'God will help me to redress that wrong; or if not me, surely he will help those that come after me. For His eternal will is, to overcome evil with good.'

The spirit of romance will never die, as long as there is a man left to see that the world might and can be better, happier, wiser, fairer in all things, than it is now. The spirit of romance will never die, as long as a man has faith in God to believe that the world will actually be better and fairer than it is now; as long as men have faith, however weak, to believe in the romance of all romances; in the wonder of all wonders; in that, of which all poets' dreams have been but childish hints, and dumb forefeelings—even

> 'That one far-off divine event
> Towards which the whole creation moves;'

that wonder of which prophets and apostles have told, each according to his light; that wonder which Habakkuk saw afar off, and foretold how that the earth should be filled with the knowledge of the Lord, as the waters cover the sea; that wonder which Isaiah saw afar off, and sang how the Lord should judge among the nations, and rebuke among many people; and they should beat their swords into plough-shares, and their spears into pruning-hooks; nation should not rise against nation, neither should they learn war any more; that wonder of which St. Paul prophesied, and said that Christ should reign till He had put all His enemies under His feet; that wonder of which St. John prophesied; and said, 'I saw the Holy City, new Jerusalem, coming down from God out of heaven. And the nations of them that are saved shall walk in the light of it, and the kings of the earth bring their glory and their honour unto it;' that wonder, finally, which our Lord Himself bade us pray for, as for our daily bread, and say, 'Father, thy kingdom come; thy will be done on earth, as it is in heaven.'

'Thy will be done on earth.' He who bade us ask that boon for generations yet unborn, was very God of very God. Do you think that He would have bidden us ask a blessing, which He knew would never come?

SERMON XIV.
THE GREAT COMMANDMENT.

MATT. xxii. 37, 38.

Thou shalt love the Lord thy God with all thy heart, and with all thy soul, and with all thy mind. This is the first and great commandment.

SOME say, when they hear this,—It is a hard saying. Who can bear it? Who can expect us to do as much as that? If we are asked to be respectable and sober, to live and let live, not to harm our neighbours wilfully or spitefully, and to come to church tolerably regularly—we understand being asked to do that—it is fair. But to love the Lord our God with all our hearts. That must be meant only for very great saints; for a few exceedingly devout people here and there. And devout people have been too apt to say,—You are right. It is we who are to love God with all our hearts and souls, and give up the world, and marriage, and all the joys of life, and turn priests, monks, and nuns, while you need only be tolerably respectable, and attend to your religious duties from time to time, while we will pray for you. But, my friends, if we read our Bibles, we cannot allow that. 'Thou shalt love the Lord thy God,' was spoken not to monks and nuns (for there were none in those days), not to great saints only (for we read of none just then), not even to priests and clergymen only. It was said to all the Jews, high and low, free and slave, soldier and labourer, alike—'Thou, a man living in the world, and doing work in the world, with wife and family, farm and cattle, horse to ride, and weapon to wear—thou shalt love the Lord thy God.'

And therefore these words are said to you and me. We English are neither monks nor nuns, nor likely (thank God) to become so. We are in the world, with our own family ties and duties, our own worldly business. And to us, to you and me, as to those old Jews, the first and great commandment is, 'Thou shalt love the Lord thy God.'

What, then, does it mean? Does it mean that we are to have the same love toward God as we have toward a wife or a husband?

Certainly not. But it means at least this—the love which we should bear toward a Father. All, my friends, turns on this. Do you look on God as your Father, or do you not? God is your Father, remember, already. You cannot (as some people seem to think) make Him your Father by believing that He is one; and you need not, thanks to His mercy. Neither can you make Him not your Father by forgetting Him. Be you wise or foolish, right or wrong, God is your Father in heaven; and you ought to feel towards Him as towards a father, not with any sentimental, fanciful, fanatical affection; but with a reverent, solemn, and rational affection; such as that which the good old Catechism bids us have, when it tells us our duty toward God.

'My duty towards God is to believe in Him, to fear Him, and to love Him with all my heart, with all my mind, with all my soul, and with all my strength; to worship Him, to give Him thanks, to put my whole trust in Him, to call upon Him, to honour His holy Name and His Word, and to serve Him truly all the days of my life.'

Now, I ask you—and what I ask you I ask myself,—Do we love the Lord our God thus? And if not, why not?

I do not ask you to tell me. I am not going to tell you what is in my heart; and I do not ask you to tell me what is in yours. We are free Englishmen, who keep ourselves to ourselves, and think for ourselves, each man in the depths of his own heart; and who are the stronger and the wiser for not talking about our feelings to any man, priest or layman.

But ask yourselves, each of you,—Do I love God? And if not, why not?

There are two reasons, I believe, which are, alas! very

common. For one of them there are great excuses; for the other, there is no excuse whatsoever.

In the first place, too many find it difficult to love God, because they have not been taught that God is loveable, and worthy of their love. They have been taught dark and hard doctrines, which have made them afraid of God.

They have been taught—too many are taught still—not merely that God will punish the wicked, but that God will punish nine-tenths, or ninety-nine-hundredths of the human race. That He will send to endless torments not merely sinners who have rebelled against what they knew was right, and His command; who have stained themselves with crimes; who wilfully injured their fellow-creatures: but that He will do the same by little children, by innocent young girls, by honourable, respectable, moral men and women, because they are not what is called sensibly converted, or else what is called orthodox. They have been taught to look on God, not as a loving and merciful Father, but as a tyrant and a task-master, who watches to set down against them the slightest mishap or neglect; who is extreme to mark what is done amiss; who wills the death of a sinner. Often—strangest notion of all—they have been told that, though God intends to punish them, they must still love Him, or they will be punished —as if such a notion, so far from drawing them to God, could do anything but drive them from Him. And it is no wonder if persons who have been taught in their youth such notions concerning God, find it difficult to love Him. Who can be frightened or threatened into loving any being? How can we love any being who does not seem to us kind, merciful, amiable, loving? Our love must be called out by God's love. If we are to love God, it must be because He has first loved us.

But He has first loved us, my friends. The dark and cruel notions about God—which are too common, and have been too common in all ages—are not what the world about us teaches, nor what Scripture teaches us either.

Look out on the world around you. What witness does it bear concerning the God who made it? Who made the sunshine, and the flowers, and singing birds, and little children, and all that causes the joy of this life? Let Christ Himself speak, and His apostles. No one can say that their words are not true; that they were mistaken in their view of this earth, or of God who gave it to us that it might bear witness of Him. What said our Lord to the poor folk of Galilee, of whom the Scribes and the Pharisees, in their pride, said, 'This people, who knoweth not the law, is accursed.'—What said our Lord, very God of very God? He told them to look on the world around, and learn from it that they had in heaven not a tyrant, not a destroyer, but a Father; a Father in heaven who is perfect in this, that He causeth His sun to shine upon them, and is good to the unthankful and the evil.

What of Him did St. Paul say?—and that not to Christians, but to heathens—That God had not left Himself without a witness even to the heathen who knew Him not—and what sort of witness? The witness of His bounty and goodness. The simple, but perpetual witness of the yearly harvest—'In that He sends men rain and fruitful seasons, filling their hearts with food and gladness.'

This is St. Paul's witness. And what is St. James's? He tells men of a Father of lights, from whom comes down every good and perfect gift; who gives to all liberally, and upbraideth not, grudges not, stints not, but gives, and delights in giving,—the same God, in a word, of whom the old psalmists and prophets spoke, and said, 'Thou openest Thine hand, and fillest all things with good.'

And if natural religion tells us thus much, and bears witness of a Father who delights in the happiness of His creatures, what does revealed religion and the Gospel of Jesus Christ tell us?

Oh, my friends, dull indeed must be our hearts if we can feel no love for the God of whom the Gospel speaks! And perverse, indeed, must be our minds if we can twist the good news of Christ's salvation into the bad news of condemnation! What says St. Paul, —That God is against us? No. But—'If God be for us, who can be against us?

'Who shall lay any thing to the charge of God's elect? It is God that justifieth. Who is he that condemneth? It is Christ that died, yea rather, that is risen again, who is even at the right hand of God, who also maketh intercession for us.

'Who shall separate us from the love of Christ? shall tribulation, or distress, or persecution, or famine, or nakedness, or peril, or sword?

'As it is written, For Thy sake we are killed all the day long; we are accounted as sheep for the slaughter.

'Nay, in all these things we are more than conquerors through Him that loved us.

'For I am persuaded, that neither death, nor life, nor angels, nor principalities, nor powers, nor things present, nor things to come, nor height, nor depth, nor any other creature, shall be able to separate us from the love of God, which is in Christ Jesus our Lord.'

What says St. John? Does he say that God the Father desires to punish or slay us; and that our Lord Jesus Christ, or the Virgin Mary, or the saints, or any other being, loves us better than God, and will deliver us out of the hands of God? God forbid! 'We have known and believed,' he says, 'the love that God hath to us. God is love, and he that dwelleth in love dwelleth in God, and God in him.'

My friends, if we could believe those blessed words—I do not say in all their fulness—we shall never do that, I believe, in this mortal life—but if we could only believe them a little, and know and believe even a little of the love that God has to us, then love to Him would spring up in our hearts, and we should feel for Him all that child ever felt for father. If we really believed that God who made heaven and earth was even now calling to each and every one of us, and beseeching us, by the sacrifice of His well-beloved Son, crucified for us, 'My son, give Me thy heart,' we could not help giving up our hearts to Him.

Provided—and there is that second reason why people do not love God, for which I said there was no excuse—provided only that we wish to be good, and to obey God. If we do not wish to do what God commands, we shall never love God. It must be so. There can be no real love of God which is not based upon a love of virtue and goodness, upon what our Lord calls a hunger and thirst after righteousness. 'If ye love Me, keep My commandments,' is our Lord's own rule and test. And it is the only one possible. If we habitually disobey any person, we shall cease to love that person. If a child is in the habit of disobeying its parents, dark and angry feelings towards those parents are sure to arise in its heart. The child tries to forget its parents, to keep out of their way. It tries to justify itself, to excuse itself by fancying that its parents are hard upon it, unjust, grudge it pleasure, or what not. If its parents' commandments are grievous to a child, it will try to make out that those commandments are unfair and unkind. And so shall we do by God's commandments. If God's commandments seem too grievous for us to obey, then we shall begin to fancy them unjust and unkind. And then, farewell to any real love to God. If we do not openly rebel against God, we shall still try to forget Him. The thought of God will seem dark, unpleasant, and forbidding to us; and we shall try, in our short-sighted folly, to live as far as we can without God in the world, and, like Adam after his fall, hide ourselves from the loving God, just because we know we have disobeyed Him.

But if, in spite of many bad habits, we desire to get rid of our bad habits; if, in spite of many faults, we still desire to be faultless and perfect; if, in spite of many weaknesses, we still desire to be strong; if, in one word, we still hunger and thirst after righteousness, and long to be good men; then, in due time, the love of God will be shed abroad in our hearts by the Holy Spirit.

For that will happen to us which happens to all those who have the pure, true, and heroical love. If we really love a person, we shall first desire to please them, and therefore the thought of disobeying and paining them will seem more and more grievous unto us.

But more. We shall soon rise a step higher. The more we love them, and the more we see in them, in their characters, things worthy to be loved, the more we shall desire to be like them, to copy those parts of their characters which most delight us; and we shall copy them: though insensibly, perhaps, and unawares.

For no one can look up for any length of time with love and respect towards a person better, wiser, greater than themselves, without becoming more or less like that person in character and in habit of thought and feeling; and so it will be with us towards God.

If we really long to be good, it will grow more and more easy to us to love God. The more pure our hearts are, the more pleasant the thought of God will be to us; even as it is said, 'Blessed are the pure in heart, for they shall see God,'—in this life as well as in the life to come. We shall not shrink from God, because we shall know that we are not wilfully offending Him.

But more. The more we think of God, the more we shall long to be like Him. How admirable in our eyes will seem His goodness, how admirable His purity, His justice, and His bounty, His long-suffering, His magnanimity and greatness of heart. For how great must be that heart of God, of which it is written, that 'He hateth nothing that He hath made, but His mercy is over all

His works;' 'that He willeth that none should perish, but that all should be saved, and come to the knowledge of the truth.' Although He be infinitely high and far off, and we cannot attain to Him, yet we shall feel it our duty and our joy to copy Him, however faintly, and however humbly; and our highest hope will be that we may behold, as in a glass, the glory of the Lord, and be changed into His image from glory to glory, even as by the Spirit of the Lord; that so, whether in this world or in the world to come, we may at last be perfect, even as our Father in heaven is perfect, and, like Him, cause the sunlight of our love to shine upon the evil and on the good; the kindly showers of our good deeds to fall upon the just and on the unjust; and—like Him who sent His only begotten Son to save the world—be good to the unthankful and to the evil.

SERMON XV.

THE EARTHQUAKE.

(Preached October 11, 1863.*)*

PSALM xlvi. 1, 2.

God is our refuge and strength, a very present help in trouble. Therefore will not we fear, though the earth be removed, and though the mountains be carried into the midst of the sea.

NO one, my friends, wishes less than I, to frighten you, or to take a dark and gloomy view of this world, or of God's dealings with men. But when God Himself speaks, men are bound to take heed, even though the message be an awful one. And last week's earthquake was an awful message, reminding all reasonable souls how frail man is, how frail his strongest works, how frail this seemingly solid earth on which we stand; what a thin crust there is between us and the nether fires, how utterly it depends on God's mercy that we do not, like Korah, Dathan, and Abiram of old, go down alive into the pit.

What do we know of earthquakes? We know that they are connected with burning mountains; that the eruption of a burning mountain is generally preceded by, and accompanied with, violent earthquakes. Indeed, the burning mountains seem to be outlets, by which the earthquake force is carried off. We know that these burning mountains give out immense volumes of steam. We know that the expanding power of steam is by far the strongest force in the world; and, therefore, it is supposed reasonably, that earthquakes are caused by steam underground.

We know concerning earthquakes two things: first, that they are quite uncertain in their effects; secondly, quite uncertain in their occurrence.

No one can tell what harm an earthquake will, or will not, do. There are three kinds. One which raises the ground up perpendicularly, and sets it down again—which is the least hurtful; one which sets it rolling in waves, like the waves of the sea—which is more hurtful; and one, the most terrible of all, which gives the ground a spinning motion, so that things thrown down by it fall twisted from right to left, or left to right. But what kind of earthquake will take place, no one can tell.

Moreover, a very slight earthquake may do fearful damage. People who only read of them, fancy that an earthquake, to destroy man and his works, must literally turn the earth upside down; that the ground must open, swallowing up houses, vomiting fire and water;

that rocks must be cast into the sea, and hills rise where valleys were before. Such awful things have happened, and will happen again: but it does not need them to lay a land utterly waste. A very slight shock —a shock only a little stronger than was felt last Wednesday morning, might have — one hardly dare think of what it might have done in a country like this, where houses are thinly built because we have no fear of earthquakes. Every manufactory and mill throughout the iron districts (where the shock was felt most) might have toppled to the earth in a moment. Whole rows of houses, hastily and thinly built, might have crumbled down like packs of cards; and hundreds of thousands of sleeping human beings might have been buried in the ruins, without time for a prayer or a cry.

A little more—a very little more—and all that or more might have happened; millions' worth of property might have been destroyed in a few seconds, and the prosperity and civilization of England have been thrown back for a whole generation. There is absolutely no reason whatever, I tell you, save the mercy of God, why that, or worse, should not have happened; and it is only of the Lord's mercies that we were not consumed.

Next, earthquakes are utterly uncertain as to time. No one knows when they are coming. They give no warning. Even in those unhappy countries in which they are most common there may not be a shock for months or years; and then a sudden shock may hurl down whole towns. Or there may be many, thirty or forty a-day for weeks, as there happened in a part of South America a few years ago, when day after day, week after week, terrible shocks went on with a perpetual underground roar, as if brass and iron were crashing and clanging under the feet, till the people were half mad with the continual noise and continual anxiety, expecting every moment one shock, stronger than the rest, to swallow them up. It is impossible, I say, to calculate when they will come. They are altogether in the hand of God,—His messengers, whose time and place He alone knows, and He alone directs.

Our having had one last week is no reason for our not having another this week, or any day this week; and no reason, happily, against our having no more for one hundred years. It is in God's hands, and in God's hands we must leave it.

All we can say is, that when one comes, it is likely to be least severe in this part of England, and most severe (like this last) in the coal and iron districts of the west and north-west, where it is easy to see that earthquakes were once common, by the cracks, twists and settlements in the rocks, and the lava streams, poured out from fiery vents (probably under water) which pierce the rocks in many places. Beyond that we know nothing, and can only say,—It is of the Lord's mercies that we are not consumed.

Why do I say these things? To frighten you? No, but to warn you. When you say to yourselves,—Earthquakes are so uncommon and so harmless in England that there is no need to think of them, you say on the whole what is true. It has been, as yet, God's will that earthquakes should be uncommon and slight in England; and therefore we have a reasonable ground of belief that such will be His will for the future. Certainly He does not wish us to fold our hands, and say, there is no use in building or improving the country, if an earthquake may come and destroy it at any moment. If there be an evil which man can neither prevent or foresee, then, if he be a wise man, he will go on as if that evil would never happen. We ever must work on in hope and in faith in God's goodness, without tormenting and weakening ourselves by fears about what may happen.

But when God gives to a whole country a distinct and solemn warning, especially after giving that country an enormous bounty in an abundant harvest, He surely means that country to take the warning. And, if I dare so judge, He means us perhaps to think of the earthquake, and somewhat in this way.

There is hardly any country in the world in which man's labour has been so successful as in England. Owing to our having no earthquakes, no really destructive storms,—and, thank God, no foreign invading armies,—the wealth of England has gone on increasing steadily and surely for centuries past, to a degree unexampled. We have never had to rebuild whole towns after an earthquake. We have never seen (except in small patches) whole districts of fertile land ruined by the sea or by floods. We have never seen every mill and house in a country blown down by a hurricane, and the crops mown off the ground by the mere force of the wind, as has happened again and again in our West India Islands. Most blessed of all, we have never seen a foreign army burning our villages, sacking our towns, carrying off our corn and cattle, and driving us into the woods to starve. From all these horrors, which have, one or other of them, fallen on almost every nation upon earth, God has of His great mercy preserved us. Ours is not the common lot of humanity. We English do not know the sorrows which average men and women go through, and have been going through, alas! ever since Adam fell. We have been an exception, a favoured and peculiar people, allowed to thrive and fatten quietly and safely for hundreds of years.

But what if that very security tempts us to forget

God? Is it not so? Are we not—I am sure I am—too apt to take God's blessings for granted, without thanking Him for them, or remembering really that He gave them, and that He can take them away? Do we not take good fortune for granted? Do we not take for granted that if we build a house it will endure for ever; that if we buy a piece of land it will be called by our name long years hence; that if we amass wealth we shall hand it down safely to our children? Of course we think we shall prosper. We say to ourselves, To-morrow shall be as to-day, and yet more abundant.

Nothing can happen to England, is, I fear, the feeling of Englishmen. Carnal security is the national sin to which we are tempted, because we have not now for forty years felt anything like national distress; and Britain says, like Babylon of old, the lady of kingdoms to whom foreigners so often compare her,—'I shall be a lady for ever; I am, there is none beside me. I shall never sit as a widow, nor know the loss of children.'

What, too, if that same security and prosperity tempts us—as foreigners justly complain of us—to set our hearts on material wealth; to believe that our life, and the life of Britain, depends on the abundance of the things which she possesses? To say—Corn and cattle, coal and iron, house and land, shipping and rail-roads, these make up Great Britain. While she has these she will endure for ever.

Ah, my friends—to people in such a temptation, is it wonderful that a good God should send a warning unmistakeable, though only a warning; most terrible, though mercifully harmless; a warning which says, in a voice which the dullest can hear—Endure for ever? The solid ground on which you stand cannot do that. Safe? Nothing on earth is safe for a moment, save in the long-suffering and tender mercy of Him of whom are all things, and by whom are all things, without whom not a sparrow falls to the ground. Is the wealth of Britain, then, what she can see and handle? The towns she builds, the roads she makes, the manufactures and goods she produces? One touch of the finger of God, and that might be all rolled into a heap of ruins, and the labour of years scattered in the dust. You trust in the sure solid earth? You shall feel it, if but for once, reel and quiver under your feet, and learn that it is not solid at all, or sure at all; that there is nothing solid, sure, or to be depended on, but the mercy of the living God; and that your solid-seeming earth on which you build is nothing less than a mine, which may bubble, and heave, and burst beneath your feet, charged for ever with an explosive force, as much more terrible than that gunpowder which you have invented to kill each other withal, as the works of God are greater than the works of man. Safe, truly! It is of God's mercy from day to day and hour to hour that we are not consumed.

This, surely, or something like this, is what the earthquake says to us. It speaks to us most gently, and yet most awfully, of a day in which the heavens may pass away with a great noise, and the elements may melt with fervent heat, and the earth and the works which are therein may be burnt up. It tells us that this is no impossible fancy: that the fires imprisoned below our feet can, and may, burst up and destroy mankind and the works of man in one great catastrophe, to which the earthquake of Lisbon in 1755—when 60,000 persons were killed, crushed, drowned, or swallowed up in a few minutes—would be a merely paltry accident.

And it bids us think, as St. Peter bids us:

'When therefore all these things are dissolved, what manner of persons ought ye to be in holy conversation and godliness?'

What manner of persons?

Remember, that if an earthquake destroyed all England, or the whole world; if this earth on which we live crumbled to dust, and were blotted out of the number of the stars, there is one thing which earthquake, and fire, and all the forces of nature cannot destroy, and that is—the human race.

We should still be. We should still endure. Not, indeed, in flesh and blood: but in some state or other;

each of us the same as now, our characters, our feelings, our goodness or our badness; our immortal spirits and very selves, unchanged, ready to receive, and certain to receive, the reward of the deeds done in the body, whether they be good or evil. Yes, we should still endure, and God and Christ would still endure. But as our Saviour, or as our Judge? That is a very awful thought.

One day or other, sooner or later, each of us shall stand before the judgment-seat of Christ, stripped of all we ever had, ever saw, ever touched, ever even imagined to ourselves, alone with our own consciences, alone with our own deserts. What shall we be saying to ourselves then?

Shall we be saying—I have lost all: The world is gone—the world, in which were set all my hopes, all my wishes; the world in which were all my pleasures, all my treasures; the world, which was the only thing I cared for, though it warned me not to trust in it, as it trembled beneath my feet? But the world is gone, and now I have nothing left!

Or, shall we be saying,—The world is gone? Then let it go. It was not a home. I took its good things as thankfully as I could. I took its sorrows and troubles as patiently as I could. But I have not set my heart on the world. My treasure, my riches, were not of the world. My peace was a peace which the world did not give, and could not take away. And now the world is gone, I keep my peace, I keep my treasure still. My peace is where it was, in my own heart. My peace is what it was: my faith in God,—faith that my sins are forgiven me for Christ's sake: my faith that God my Father loves me, and cares for me; and that nothing,—height or depth, or time or space, or life or death, can part me from His love: my faith that I have not been quite useless in the world; that I have tried to do my duty in my place; and that the good which I have done, little as it has been, will not go forgotten by that merciful God, by whose help it was done, who rewards all men according to the works which He gives them heart to perform. And my treasure is where it was—in my heart; and what it was, —the Holy Spirit of God, the spirit of goodness, of faith and truth, of mercy and justice, of love to God and love to man, which is everlasting life itself. That I have. That time cannot abate, nor death abolish, nor the world, nor the destruction of the world, nor of all worlds, can take away.

Choose, my friends, which of these two frames of mind would you rather be in when the great day of the Lord comes, foretold by that earthquake, and by all earthquakes that ever were.

Will you be then like those whom St. John saw calling on the mountains to fall on them, and the hills to hide them from the wrath of Him that sat on the throne, and from the anger of the Lamb?

Or will you be like him who saith—God is my hope and strength, my present help in trouble. Therefore will I not fear, though the earth be shaken, and though the mountains be carried into the depth of the sea?

SERMON XVI.

THE METEOR SHOWER.

(Preached at the Chapel Royal, St. James's, Nov. 26, 1866.)

St. Matthew x. 29, 30.

Are not two sparrows sold for a farthing? and one of them shall not fall on the ground without your Father. But the very hairs of your head are all numbered.

IT will be well for us to recollect, once for all, who spoke these words; even Jesus Christ, who declared that He was one with God the Father; Jesus Christ, whom His apostles declared to be the Creator of the universe. If we believe this, as Christian men, it will be well for us to take our Lord's account of a universe which He Himself created; and to believe that in the most minute occurrence of nature, there is a special providence, by which not a sparrow falls to the ground without our Father.

I confess that it is difficult to believe this heartily. It was never anything but difficult. In the earliest ages, those who first thought about the universe found it so difficult that they took refuge in the fancy of a special providence which was administered by the planets above their heads, and believed that the affairs of men, and of the world on which they lived, were ruled by the aspects of the sun and moon, and the host of heaven.

Men found it so difficult in the Middle Age, that they took refuge in the fancy of a special providence administered by certain demi-gods whom they called 'The Saints;' and believed that each special disease, or accident, was warded off from mankind, from their cattle, or from their crops, by a special saint who overlooked their welfare.

Men find it so difficult now-a-days, that the great majority of civilized people believe in no special providence at all, and take refuge in the belief that the universe is ruled by something which they call law.

Therein, doubtless, they have hold of a great truth; but one which will be only half-true, and therefore injurious, unless it be combined with other truths; unless questions are answered which too many do not care to answer: as, for instance,—Can there be a law without a law-giver? Can a law work without one who administers the law? Are not the popular phrases of 'laws impressed on matter,' 'laws inherent in matter,' mere metaphors, dangerous, because inaccurate; confirmed as little by experience and reason, as by Scripture?

Does not all law imply a will? Does not an Almighty Will imply a special providence?

But these are questions for which most persons have neither time nor inclination. Indeed, the whole matter is unimportant to them. They have no special need of a special providence. Their lives and properties are very safe in this civilized country; and their secret belief is that, whatever influence God may have on the next world, He has little or no influence on this world; neither on the facts of nature, nor on the events of history, nor on the course of their own lives; and that a special providence seems to them—if they dare confess as much—an unnecessary superstition.

Only poor folk in cottages and garrets—and a few more who are, happily, poor in spirit, though not in purse—grinding amid the iron facts of life, and learning there by little sound science, it may be, but much sound theology—still believe that they have a Father in heaven, before whom the very hairs of their head are all numbered; and that if they had not, then this would not only be a bad world, but a mad world likewise; and that it were better for them that they had never been born.

Nevertheless, it is difficult to believe in the special providence of our Father in heaven. Difficult: though necessary. Just as it is difficult to believe that the earth moves round the sun. Contrary, like that fact, to a great deal of our seeming experience.

It is easy enough, of course, to believe that our Father sends what is plainly good. Not so easy to believe that He sends what at least seems evil.

Easy enough, when we see spring-time and harvest, sunshine and flowers, to say—Here are 'acts of God's providence.' Not so easy, when we see blight and pestilence, storm and earthquake, to say,—Here are 'acts of God's providence' likewise.

For this innumerable multitude of things, of which we now-a-days talk as if it were one thing, and had an organic unity of its own, or even as if it were one person, and had a will of its own, and call it Nature—a word which will one day be forgotten by philosophers, with the 'four elements,' and the 'animal spirits;'—this multitude of things, I say, which we miscall Nature, has its dark and ugly, as well as its bright and fair side. Nature, says some one, is like the spotted panther— most playful, and yet most treacherous; most beautiful, and yet most cruel. It acts at times after a fashion most terrible, undistinguishing, wholesale, seemingly pitiless. It seems to go on its own way, as in a storm or an earthquake, careless of what it crushes. Terrible enough Nature looks to the savage, who thinks it crushes him from mere caprice. More terrible still does Science make Nature look, when she tells us that it crushes, not by caprice, but by brute necessity; not by ill-will, but by inevitable law. Science frees us in many ways (and all thanks to her) from the bodily terror which the savage feels. But she replaces that, in the minds of many, by a moral terror which is far more overwhelming. Am I —a man is driven to ask—am I, and all I love, the victims of an organised tyranny, from which there can be no escape—for there is not even a tyrant from whom I may perhaps beg mercy? Are we only helpless particles, at best separate parts of the wheels of a vast machine, which will use us till it has worn us away, and ground us to powder? Are our bodies—and if so, why not our souls?—the puppets, yea, the creatures of necessary circumstances, and all our strivings and sorrows only vain beatings against the wires of our cage, cries of 'Why hast thou made me, then?' which are addressed to nothing? Tell us not that the world is governed by universal law; the news is not comfortable, but simply horrible, unless you can tell us, or allow others to tell us, that there is a loving giver, and a just administrator of that law.

Horrible, I say, and increasingly horrible, not merely to the sentimentalist, but to the man of sound reason and of sound conscience, must the scientific aspect of nature become, if a mere abstraction called law is to be the sole ruler of the universe; if—to quote the famous words of the German sage—'If, instead of the Divine Eye, there must glare on us an empty, black, bottomless eye-socket;' and the stars and galaxies of heaven, in spite of all their present seeming regularity, are but an 'everlasting storm which no man guides.'

It was but a few days ago that we, and this little planet on which we live, caught a strange and startling glimpse of that everlasting storm which—shall I say it? —no one guides.

We were swept helpless, astronomers tell us, through a cloud of fiery stones, to which all the cunning bolts which man invents to slay his fellow-man, are but slow and weak engines of destruction.

We were free from the superstitious terror with which that meteor-shower would have been regarded in old times. We could comfort ourselves, too, with the fact that heaven's artillery was not known as yet to have killed any one; and with the scientific explanation of that fact, namely, that most of the bolts were small enough to be melted and dissipated by their rush through our atmosphere.

But did the thought occur to none of us, how morally ghastly, in spite of all its physical beauty, was that grand sight, unless we were sure that behind it all, there was a living God? Unless we believed that not one of those bolts fell, or did not fall to the ground without our Father? That He had appointed the path, and the time, and the destiny, and the use of every atom of that matter, of which science could only tell us that it was rushing without a purpose, for ever through the homeless void?

We may believe that, mind, without denying scientific laws, or their permanence in any way. It is not a question, this, of a living God, whether He interferes with His own laws now and then, but whether interference is not the law of all laws itself. It is not a question of special providences here and there, in favour of this person or that; but whether the whole universe and its history is not one perpetual and innumerable series of special providences. Whether the God who ordained the laws is not so administering them, so making them interfere with, balance, and modify each other, as to cause them to work together perpetually for good; so that every minutest event (excepting always the sin and folly of rational beings) happens in the place, time, and manner, where it is specially needed. In one word, the question is not whether there be a God, but whether there be a living God, who is in any true and practical sense Master of the universe over which He presides; a King who is actually ruling His kingdom, or an Epicurean deity who lets his kingdom rule itself.

Is there a living God in the universe, or is there none? That is the greatest of all questions. Has our Lord Jesus Christ answered it, or has He not? Easy, well-to-do people, who find this world pleasant, and whose chief concern is to live till they die, care little about that question. This world suits them well enough, whether there be a living God or not; and as for the next world, they will be sure to find some preacher or confessor who will set their minds easy about it.

Fanatics and bigots, of all denominations, care little about that question. For they say in their hearts— 'God is our Father, whosesoever Father He is not. We are His people, and God performs acts of providence for us. But as for the people outside, who know not the law, nor the Gospel, either, they are accursed. It is not our concern to discuss whether God performs acts of providence for them.'

But here and there, among rich and poor, there are those whose heart and flesh—whose conscience and whose intellect—cry out for the living God, and will know no peace till they have found Him.

A living God; a true God; a real God; a God worthy of the name; a God who is working for ever, everywhere, and in all; who hates nothing that He has made, forgets nothing, neglects nothing; a God who satisfies not only their heads, but their hearts; not only their logical intellects, but their higher reason—that pure reason, which is one with the conscience and moral sense. For Him they cry out; Him they seek: and if they cannot find Him they know no rest. For then they can find no explanation of the three great human questions—Where am I? Whither am I going? What must I do?

Men come to them and say, 'Of course there is a God. He created the world long ago, and set it spinning ever since by unchangeable laws.' But they answer, 'That may be true; but I want more. I want the living God.'

Other men come to them and say, 'Of course there is a God; and when the universe is destroyed, He will save a certain number of the elect, or orthodox. Do you take care that you are among that number, and leave the rest to Him.' But they answer, 'That may be true; but I want more. I want the living God.'

They will say so very confusedly. They will often not be able to make men understand their meaning. Nay, they will say and do—driven by despair—very unwise things. They will even fall down and worship the Holy Bread in the Sacrament of the Lord's Supper, and say, 'The living God is in that. You have forbidden us, with your theories, to find the living God either in heaven or earth. But somewhere He must be. And in despair, we will fall back upon the old belief that He is in the wafer on the altar, and find there Him whom our souls must find, or be for ever without a home.' Strange and sad, that that should be the last outcome of the century of mechanical philosophy. But before we blame the doctrine as materialistic,—which, I fear, it too truly is,—we should remember that, for the last fifty years, the young have been taught more and more to be materialists; that they have been taught more and more to believe in a God who rules over Sundays, but not over week-day business; over the next world, but not over this; a God, in short, in whom men do not live, and move, and have their being. They have been brought up, I say, unconsciously, but surely, as practical materialists, who make their senses the ground of all their knowledge; and therefore, when a revulsion happens to them, they are awakened to look for the living God—they look for him instinctively in visible matter.

But for the living God thoughtful men will look more and more. Physical science is forcing on them the question, Do we live, and move, and have our being in God? Is there a real and perpetual communication between the visible and the invisible world, or is there not? Are all the beliefs of man, from the earliest ages, that such there was, dreams and nothing more? Is any religion whatsoever to be impossible henceforth? And to find an answer, men will go, either backward to superstition, or forward into pantheism; for in atheism, whether practical or theoretical, they cannot abide.

The Bible says that those old beliefs, however partial or childish, were no dreams, but instincts of an eternal truth; that there is such a communication between the universe and the living God. Prophets, Psalmists, Apostles, speak—like our Nicene Creed—of a Spirit of God, the Lord and Giver of Life, in words which are not pantheism, but are the very deliverance from pantheism, because they tell us that that Spirit proceeds, not merely from a Deity, not merely from a Creator, but from a Father in heaven, and from a Son who is His likeness and His Word.

And from this ground Natural Theology must start, if it is ever to revive again, instead of remaining, as now, an extinct science. It must begin from the keyword of the text, 'Your Father.' As long as Natural Theology begins from nature, and not from God Himself, it will inevitably drift into pantheism, as Pope drifted, in spite of himself, when he tried to look from nature up to nature's God. As long as men speculate on the dealings of a Deity or of a Creator, they will find out nothing, because they are searching under the wrong name, and therefore, as logicians will tell you, for the wrong thing.

But when they begin to seek under the right name—the name which our Lord revealed to the debased multitudes of Judæa, when He told them that not a sparrow fell to the ground without—not the Deity, not the Creator, but their Father; then, in God's good time, all may come clear once more.

This at least will come clear,—a doubt which often presents itself to the mind of scientific men.

This earth—we know now that it is not the centre, not the chief body, of the universe, but a tiny planet, a speck, an atom among millions of bodies far vaster than itself.

It was credible enough in old times, when the earth was held to be all but the whole universe, that God should descend on earth, and take on. Him human nature, to save human beings. Is it credible now? This little corner of the systems and the galaxies? This paltry race which we call man? Are they worthy of the interposition, of the death, of Incarnate God—of the Maker of such a universe as Science has discovered?

Yes. If we will keep in mind that one word 'Father.' Then we dare say Yes, in full assurance of Faith. For then we have taken the question off the mere material ground of size and of power; to put it once and for ever on that spiritual ground of justice and love, which is implied in the one word—'Father.'

If God be a perfect Father, then there must be a perpetual intercourse of some kind between Him and His children; between Him and that planet, however small, on which He has set His children, that they may be educated into His likeness. If God be perfect justice, the wrong, and consequent misery of the universe, however small, must be intolerable to Him. If God be perfect love, there is no sacrifice—remember that great word—which He may not condescend to make, in order to right that wrong, and alleviate that misery. If God be the Father of our spirits, the spiritual welfare of His children may be more important to Him than the fate of the whole brute matter of the universe. Think not to frighten us with the idols of size and height. God is a Spirit, before whom all material things are equally great, and equally small. Let us think of Him as such, and not merely as a Being of physical power and inventive craft. Let us believe in our Father in heaven. For then that higher intellect,—that pure reason, which dwells not in the heads, but in the hearts of men, will tell them that if they have a Father in heaven, He must be exercising a special providence over the minutest affairs of their lives, by which He is striving to educate them into His likeness; a special providence over the fate of every atom in the universe, by which His laws shall work together for the moral improvement of every creature capable thereof; that not a sparrow can fall to the ground without his knowledge; and that not a hair of their head can be touched, unless suffering is needed for the education of their souls.

SERMON XVII.

CHOLERA, 1866.

LUKE vii. 16.

There came a fear on all: and they glorified God, saying, That a great prophet is risen up among us; and, That God hath visited his people.

YOU recollect to what the text refers? How the Lord visited His people? By raising to life a widow's son at Nain. That was the result of our Lord's visit to the little town of Nain. It is worth our while to think of that text, and of that word, 'visit,' just now. For we are praying to God to remove the cholera from this land. We are calling it a visitation of God; and saying that God is visiting our sins on us thereby. And we are saying the exact truth. We are using the right and scriptural word.

We know that this cholera comes by no miracle, but by natural causes. We can more or less foretell where it will break out. We know how to prevent its breaking out at all, save in a scattered case here and there. Of this there is no doubt whatsoever in the mind of any well-informed person.

But that does not prevent its being a visitation of God; yea, in most awful and literal earnest, a house-to-house visitation. God uses the powers of nature to do His work: of Him it is written, 'He maketh the winds His angels, and flames of fire His ministers.' And so this minute and invisible cholera-seed is the minister of God, by which He is visiting from house to house, searching out and punishing certain persons who have been guilty, knowingly or not, of the offence of dirt; of filthy and careless habits of living; and especially, as has long been known by well-informed men, of drinking poisoned water. Their sickness, their deaths, are God's judgment on that act of theirs, whereby God says to men,—You shall not drink water unfit for even dumb animals; and if you do, you shall die.

To this view there are two objections. First, the poor people themselves are not in fault, but those who supply poisoned water, and foul dwellings.

True: but only half true. If people demanded good water and good houses, there would soon be a supply of them. But there is not a sufficient supply; because too many of the labouring classes in towns, though they are earning very high wages, are contented to live in a condition unfit for civilized men; and of course, if they are contented so to do, there will be plenty of covetous or careless landlords who will supply the bad article with which they are satisfied; and they will be punished by disease for not having taken care of themselves.

But as for the owners of filthy houses, and the suppliers of poisoned water, be sure that, in His own way and His own time, God will visit them; that when He maketh inquisition for blood, He will assuredly requite upon the guilty persons, whoever they are, the blood of those five or six thousand of her Majesty's subjects who have been foully done to death by cholera in the last two months, as He requited the blood of Naboth, or of any other innocent victim of whom we read in Holy Writ. This outbreak of cholera in London, considering what we now know about it, and have known for twenty years past, is a national shame, scandal, and sin, which, if man cannot and will not punish, God can and will.

But there is another objection, which is far more important and difficult to answer. This cholera has not slain merely fathers and mothers of families, who were more or less responsible for the bad state of their dwellings; but little children, aged widows, and many other persons who cannot be blamed in the least.

True. And we must therefore believe that to them— indeed to all—this has been a visitation not of anger but of love. We must believe that they are taken away from some evil to come; that God permits the destruction of their bodies, to the saving of their souls. His laws are inexorable; and yet He hateth nothing that He hath made.

And we must believe that this cholera is an instance of the great law, which fulfils itself again and again, and will to the end of the world,—'It is expedient that one die for the people, and that the whole nation perish not.'

For the same dirt which produces cholera now and then, is producing always, and all day long, stunted and diseased bodies, drunkenness, recklessness, misery, and sin of all kinds; and the cholera will be a blessing, a cheap price to have paid, for the abolition of the evil spirit of dirt.

And thus much for this very painful subject—of which some of you may say—'What is it to us? We cannot prevent cholera; and, blessed as we are with abundance of the purest water, there is little or no fear of cholera ever coming into our parish.'

That last is true, my friends, and you may thank God for it. Meanwhile, take this lesson at least home with you, and teach it your children day by day—that filthy, careless, and unwholesome habits of living are in the sight of Almighty God so terrible an offence, that He sometimes finds it necessary to visit them with a severity with which He visits hardly any sin; namely, by inflict- ing capital punishment on thousands of His beloved creatures.

But though we have not had the cholera among us, has God therefore not visited us? That would surely be evil news for us, according to Holy Scripture. For if God do not visit us, then He must be far from us. But the Psalmist cries, 'Go not far from me, O Lord.' His fear is, again and again, not that God should visit him, but that God should desert him. And more, the word which is translated 'to visit,' in Scripture has the sense of seeing to a man, overseeing him, being his bishop. If God do not see to, oversee us, and be our bishop, then He must turn His face from us, which is what the Psalmist beseeches Him again and again not to do; praying, 'Hide not Thy face from me, O Lord,' and crying out of the depths of anxiety and trouble, 'Put thy trust in God, for I shall yet give Him thanks for the light of His countenance;' and again, 'In Thy presence is'—not death, but—'life; at Thy right hand is fulness of days for evermore.' And again, the Psalmist prays to God to visit him, and visit his thoughts,—'Search me, O Lord, and try the ground of my heart. Search me, and examine my thoughts. Look well if there be any wickedness in me, and lead me in the way everlasting.' Shall we pray that prayer, my friends? Shall we, with the Psalmist, pray God to visit, and, if need be, chasten and correct what He sees wrong in us? Or shall we, with the superstitious, pray to God not to visit us? to keep away from us? to leave us alone? to forget us? If He did answer that foolish prayer, there would be an end of us and all created things; for in God they live and move and have their being—as it is written, 'When Thou hidest thy face, they are troubled; when Thou takest away their breath, they die, and are turned again to their dust.' But, happily for us, God will not answer that foolish prayer. For it is written, 'If I go up to heaven, Thou art there; if I go down to hell, Thou art there also.' Nowhither can we go from God's presence: nowhither can we flee from His Spirit.

This is the Scripture language. Is ours like it? Have we not got to think of a visitation of God as a simple calamity? If a man die suddenly and strangely, he has died by the visitation of God. But if he be saved from death strangely and suddenly, it does not occur to us to call that a visitation, and to say with Scripture, 'The Lord has visited the man with His salvation.' If the cholera comes, or the crops fail, we say,—God is visiting us. If we have an especially healthy year, or a glorious harvest, we never say with Scripture, 'The Lord has visited His people in giving them bread.' Yet Scripture, if it says, 'I will visit their transgressions,' says also that the Lord visited the children of Israel to deliver them out of Egypt. If it talks of death as the visitation of all men, it speaks of God visiting Sarah and Hannah to give them children.

If it says, 'I will visit the blood shed in Jezreel,' it says also, 'Thy visitation hath preserved my spirit.' If it says, 'At the time they are visited they shall be cast down,' it says also, 'The Lord shall visit them, and turn away their captivity.'

If we look through Scripture, we find that the words 'visit' and 'visitation' are used about ninety times: that in about fifty of them the meaning of the words is chastisement of some kind or other: in about forty it is mercy and blessing: and that in the New Testament the words never mean anything but mercy and blessing, though we have begun of late years to use them only in the sense of punishment and a curse.

Now, how is this, my friends? How is it that we, who are not under the terrors of the Law, but under the Gospel of grace, have quite lost the Gospel meaning of this word 'visitation,' and take a darker view of it than did even the old Jews under the Law? Have we, whom God hath visited, indeed, in the person of His only-begotten Son Jesus Christ, any right or reason to think worse of a visitation of God than had the Jews of old? God forbid. And yet we do so, I fear; and show daily that we do so by our use of the word: for out of the abundance of the heart man's mouth speaketh. By his words he is justified, and by his words he is condemned; and there is no surer sign of what a man's real belief is, than the sense in which he naturally, as it were by instinct, uses certain words.

And what is the cause?

Shall I say it? If I do, I blame not you more than I blame myself, more than I blame this generation. But it seems to me that there is a little—or not a little —atheism among us now-a-days; that we are growing to be 'without God in the world.' We are ready enough to believe that God has to do with the next world: but we are not ready to believe that He has to do with this world. We, in this generation, do not believe that in God we live, and move, and have our being. Nay, some object to capital punishment, because (so they say) 'it hurries men into the presence of their Maker;' as if a human being could be in any better or safer place than the presence of his Maker; and as if his being there depended on us, or on any man, and not on God Almighty alone, who is surely not so much less powerful than an earthly monarch, that He cannot keep out of His presence or in it whomsoever He chooses. When we talk of being 'ushered into the presence of God,' we mean dying; as if we were not all in the presence of God at this moment, and all day long. When we say, 'Prepare to meet thy God,' we mean 'Prepare to die;' as if we did not meet our God every time we had the choice between doing a right thing and doing a wrong one—between yielding to our own lusts

and tempers, and yielding to the Holy Spirit of God.
For if the Holy Spirit of God be, as the Christian faith
tells us, God indeed, do we not meet God every time
a right, and true, and gracious thought arises in our
hearts? But we have all forgotten this, and much more
connected with this; and our notion of this world is
not that of Holy Scripture—of that grand 104th Psalm,
for instance, which sets forth the Spirit of God as the
Lord and Giver of life to all creation : but our notion is
this—that this world is a machine, which would go on
very well by itself, if God would but leave it alone;
that if the course of nature, as we atheistically call it, is
not interfered with, then suns shine, crops grow, trade
flourishes, and all is well, because God does not visit
the earth. Ah! blind that we are; blind to the power
and glory of God which is around us, giving life and
breath to all things,—God, without whom not a sparrow
falls to the ground,—God, who visiteth the earth, and
maketh it very plenteous,—God, who giveth to all liberally, and upbraideth not,—God, whose ever-creating and
ever-sustaining Spirit is the source, not only of all goodness, virtue, knowledge, but of all life, health, order,
fertility. We see not God's witness in His sending
rain and fruitful seasons, filling our hearts with food and
gladness. And then comes the punishment. Because
we will not keep up a wholesome and trustful belief in
God in prosperity, we are awakened out of our dream

of unbelief, to an unwholesome and mistrustful belief in Him in adversity. Because we will not believe in a God of love and order, we grow to believe in a God of anger and disorder. Because we will not fear a God who sends fruitful seasons, we are grown to dread a God who sends famine and pestilence. Because we will not believe in the Father in heaven, we grow to believe in a destroyer who visits from heaven. But we believe in Him only as the destroyer. We have forgotten that He is the Giver, the Creator, the Redeemer. We look on His visitations as something dark and ugly, instead of rejoicing in the thought of God's presence, as we should, if we had remembered that He was about our path and about our bed, and spying out all our ways, whether for joy or for sorrow. We shrink at the thought of His presence. We look on His visitations as things not to be understood; not to be searched out in childlike humility—and yet in childlike confidence—that we may understand why they are sent, and what useful lesson our Father means us to learn from them: but we look on them as things to be merely prayed against, if by any means God will, as soon as possible, cease to visit us, and leave us to ourselves, for we can earn our own bread comfortably enough, if it were not for His interference and visitations. We are too like the Gadarenes of old, to whom it mattered little that the Lord had restored the madman to health and reason, if He caused their swine to perish in the lake. They were uneasy and terrified at such visitations of God incarnate. He seemed to them a terrible and dangerous Being, and they besought Him to depart out of their coasts.

It would have been wiser, surely, in those Gadarenes, and better for them, had they cried—'Lord, what wilt Thou have us to do? We see that Thou art a Being of infinite power, for mercy, and for punishment likewise. And Thou art the very Being whom we want, to teach us our duty, and to make us do it. Tell us what we ought to do, and help us, and, if need be, compel us to do it, and so to prosper indeed.' And so should we pray in the case of this cholera. We may ask God to take it away: but we are bound to ask God also, why He has sent it. Till then we have no reason to suppose that He will take it away; we have no reason to suppose that it will be merciful in Him to take it away, till He has taught us why it was sent. This question of cholera has come now to a crisis, in which we must either learn why cholera comes, or incur, I hold, lasting disgrace and guilt. And—if I may dare to hint at the counsels of God—it seems as if the Almighty Lord had no mind to relieve us of that disgrace and guilt.

For months past we have been praying that this cholera should not enter England, and our prayers have not been heard. In spite of them the cholera has come; and has slain thousands, and seems likely to slay thousands more. What plainer proof can there be to those who believe in the providence of God, and the rule of Jesus Christ our Lord, than that we are meant to learn some wholesome lesson from it, which we have not learnt yet? It cannot be that God means us to learn the physical cause of cholera, for that we have known these twenty years. Foul lodging, foul food, and, above all, natural and physical, foul water; there is no doubt of the cause. But why cannot we save English people from the curse and destruction which all this foulness brings? That is the question. That is our national scandal, shame, and sin at this moment. Perhaps the Lord wills that we should learn that; learn what is the moral and spiritual cause of our own miserable weakness, negligence, hardness of heart, which, sinning against light and knowledge, has caused the death of thousands of innocent souls. God grant that we may learn that lesson. God grant that He may put into the hearts and minds of some man or men, the wisdom and courage to deliver us from such scandals for the future.

But I have little hope that that will happen, till we get rid of our secret atheism; till we give up the notion that God only visits now and then, to disorder and destroy His own handiwork, and take back the old scriptural notion, that God is visiting all day long for ever, to give order and life to His own work, to set it right whenever it goes wrong, and re-create it whenever it decays. Till then we can expect only explanations of cholera and of God's other visitations of affliction, which are so superstitious, so irrational, so little connected with the matter in hand, that they would be ridiculous, were they not somewhat blasphemous. But when men arise in this land who believe truly in an ever-present God of order, revealed in His Son Jesus Christ; when men shall arise in this land, who will believe that faith with their whole hearts, and will live and die for it and by it; acting as if they really believed that in God we live, and move, and have our being; as if they really believed that they were in the kingdom and rule of Christ,—a rule of awful severity, and yet of perfect love,—a rule, meanwhile, which men can understand, and are meant to understand, that they may not only obey the laws of God, but know the mind of God, and copy the dealings of God, and do the will of God; and when men arise in this land, who have that holy faith in their hearts, and courage to act upon it, then cholera will vanish away, and the physical and moral causes of a hundred other evils which torment poor human beings through no anger of God, but simply through their own folly, and greediness, and ignorance.

All these shall vanish away, in the day when the knowledge of the Lord shall cover the land, and men shall say, in spirit and in truth, as Christ their Lord has said before,—'Sacrifice and burnt-offering thou wouldest not. Then said I, Lo, I come. In the volume of the book it is written of Me, that I should do the will of God.' And in those days shall be fulfilled once more, the text which says,—'That the people glorified God, saying, A great Prophet, even Christ the Lord Himself, hath risen up among us, and God hath visited His people.'

SERMON XVIII.

THE WICKED SERVANT.

St. Matthew xviii. 23.

The kingdom of heaven is likened to a certain king, which would take account of his servants.

THIS parable, which you heard in the Gospel for this day, you all know. And I doubt not that all you who know it, understand it well enough. It is so human and so humane; it is told with such simplicity, and yet with such force and brilliancy that—if one dare praise our Lord's words as we praise the words of men—all must see its meaning at once, though it speaks of a state of society different from anything which we have ever seen, or, thank God, ever shall see.

The Eastern despotic king who has no law but his own will; who puts his servant—literally his slave—into a post of such trust and honour, that the slave can misappropriate and make away with the enormous sum of ten thousand talents; who commands, not only him, but his wife and children to be sold to pay the debt; who then forgives him all out of a sudden burst of pity, and again, when the wretched man has shown himself base and cruel, unworthy of that pity, revokes his pardon, and delivers him to the tormentors till he shall pay all—all this is a state of things impossible in a free country, though it is possible enough still in many countries of the East, which are governed in this very despotic fashion; and justice, and very often injustice likewise, is done in this rough, uncertain way, by the will of the king alone.

But, however different the circumstances, yet there is a lesson in this story which is universal and eternal, true for all men, and true for ever. The same human nature, for good and for evil, is in us, as was in that Eastern king and his slave. The same kingdom of heaven is over us as was over them, its laws punishing sinners by their own sins; the same Spirit of God which strove with their hearts is striving with ours. If it was not so, the parable would mean nothing to us. It would be a story of men who belonged to another moral world, and were under another moral law, not to be judged by our rules of right and wrong; and therefore a story of men whom we need not copy.

But it is not so. If the parable be—as I take for granted it is—a true story; then it was Christ, the Light who lights every man who cometh into the world, who put into that king's heart the divine feeling of mercy, and inspired him to forgive, freely and utterly, the wretched slave who worshipped him, kneeling with his forehead to the ground, and promising, in his terror, what he probably knew he could not perform—'Lord, have patience with me, and I will pay thee all.'

And it was Christ, the Light of men, who inspired that king with the feeling, not of mere revenge, but of just retribution; who taught him that, when the slave was unworthy of his mercy, he had a right, in a noble and divine indignation, to withdraw his mercy; and not to waste his favours on a bad man, who would only turn them to fresh bad account, but to keep them for those who had justice and honour enough in their hearts to forgive others, when their Lord had forgiven them.

We must bear in mind, that the king must have been right, and acting (whether he knew it or not) by the Spirit of God; else his conduct would never have been likened to the kingdom of heaven: that is, to the laws by which God governs both this world and the world to come.

The kingdom of heaven. The kingdom of God—Would that men would believe in them a little more! It seems, at times, as if all belief in them was dying out; as if men, throughout all civilized and Christian countries, had made up their minds to say—There is no kingdom of God or of heaven. There will be one hereafter, in the next world. This world is the kingdom of men, and of what they can do for themselves without God's help, and without God's laws.

My friends, the Jewish rulers of old said so, and cried, 'We have no king but Cæsar.' And they remain an example to all time, of what happens to those who deny the kingdom of God. Christ came to tell them that the kingdom of heaven was at hand, and the kingdom of God was among them. But they would have none of it. And what said our Lord of them and their notion? 'The prince of this world,' said He, 'cometh, and hath nothing in me. This is your hour and the power of darkness.' Yes; the hour in which men had determined to manage the world in their way, and not in Christ's, was also the hour of the power of darkness. That was what they had gained by having their own way; by saying—The kingdom is ours, and not God's. They had fallen under the power of darkness, not of light. The very light within them was darkness. They utterly mistook their road on earth. At the very moment that they were trying to make peace with the Roman governor, by denying that Christ was their King, and demanding that He should be crucified, —at that very moment the things which belonged to their peace were hid from their eyes. Never men made so fatal a mistake, when they thought themselves most politic and prudent. They said among themselves—'Unless we put down this man, the Romans will come and take away our place,' *i.e.* our privileges, and power, and our nation.' And what followed? That the Romans did come and take away their place and nation, with horrible massacre and ruin: and so they lost both the kingdom of this world, and the kingdom of God likewise. Never, I say, did men make a more fatal mistake in the things of this world than those Jews to whom the kingdom of God came, and they rejected it.

And so shall we, my friends, if we forget that, whether we like it or not, the kingdom of God is within us, and we within it likewise.

1. The kingdom of God is within us. Every gracious motive, every noble, just, and merciful instinct within us, is a sign to us that the kingdom of God is come to us; that we are not as the brutes which perish; not as the heathen who are too often past feeling, being alienated from the life of God by reason of the ignorance which is in them: but that we are God's children, inheritors of the kingdom of heaven; and that God's Spirit is teaching us the laws of that kingdom; so that in every child who is baptized, educated, and civilized, is fulfilled the promise, 'I will write my laws upon their hearts, and I will be to them a Father.'

God's Spirit is teaching our hearts as He taught the heart of that old Eastern king. It may be, it ought to be, that He is teaching us far deeper lessons than He ever taught that king.

2. We are in the kingdom of God. It is worth our while to remember that steadfastly just now. Many people are ready to agree that the kingdom of God is within them. They will readily confess that religion is a spiritual matter, and a matter of the heart: but their fancy is that therefore religion, and all just and noble and beautiful instincts and aspirations, are very good things for those who have them: but that, if any one has them not, it does not much matter.

They do not see that there are not only such things as feelings about God; but that there are also such things as laws of God; and that God can enforce those laws, and does enforce them, sometimes in a very terrible manner. They do not believe enough in a living God, an acting God, a God who will not merely write His laws in our hearts, if we will let Him, but may also destroy us off the face of the earth, if we would not let Him. They fancy that God either cannot, or will not, enforce His own laws, but leaves a man free to accept them, or reject as he will. There is no greater mistake. Be not deceived; God is not mocked. As a man sows, so shall he reap. God says to us, to all men,—Copy Me. Do as I do, and be My children, and be blest. But if we will not; if, after all God's care and love, the tree brings forth no fruit, then, soon or late, the sentence goes forth against it in God's kingdom, 'Cut it down; why cumbereth it the ground?'

There is a saying now-a-days, that nations and tribes who will not live reasonable lives, and behave as men should to their fellow-men, must be civilized off the face of the earth. The words are false, if they mean that we, or any other men, have a right to exterminate their fellow-creatures. But they are true, and more true than the people who use them fancy, if they are spoken not of man, but of God. For if men will not obey the laws of God's kingdom, God does actually civilize them off the face of the earth. Great nations, learned churches, powerful aristocracies, ancient institutions, has God civilized off the face of the earth before now. Because they would not acknowledge God for their King, and obey the laws of His kingdom, in which alone are life, and wealth, and health, God has taken His kingdom away from them, and given it to others who would bring forth the fruits thereof. The Jews are the most awful and famous example of that terrible judgment of God, but they are not the only ones. It has happened again and again. It may happen to you or me, as well as to this whole nation of England, if we forget that we are in God's kingdom, and that only by living according to God's laws can we keep our place therein.

And this is what the parable teaches us. The king tries to teach the servant one of the laws of his kingdom —that he rules according to boundless mercy and generosity. God wishes to teach us the same. The king does so, not by word, but by deed, by actually forgiving the man his debt. So does God forgive us freely in Jesus Christ our Lord.

But more than this, he wishes the servant to understand that he is to copy his king; that if his king has behaved to him like a father to his child, he must behave as a brother to his fellow-servants. So does God wish to teach us.

But he does not tell the man so, in so many words. He does not say to him, I command thee to forgive thy debtors as I have forgiven thee. He leaves the man to his own sense of honour and good feeling. It is a question not of the law, but of the heart. So does God with us. He educates us, not as children or slaves, but as free men, as moral agents. He leaves us to our own reason and conscience, to reap the fruit which we ourselves have sown. Therefore, about a thousand matters in life He lays on us no special command. He leaves us to act according to our good feeling, to our own sense of honour. It is a matter, I say, of the heart. If God's law be written in our hearts, our hearts will lead us to do the right thing. If God's law be not in our hearts, then mere outward commands will not make us do right, for what we do will not be really right and good, because it will not be done heartily and of our own will.

But the servant does not follow his lord's example.

Fresh from his lord's presence, he takes his fellow-servant by the throat, saying—Pay me that thou owest. His heart has not been touched. His lord's example has not softened him. He does not see how beautiful, how noble, how divine, generosity and mercy are. He is a hard-hearted, worldly man. The heavenly kingdom, which is justice and love, is not within him. Then, if the kingdom of heaven is not in him, he shall find out that he is in it; and that in a very terrible way :—

'Thou wicked servant, unworthy of my pity, because there is no goodness in thine own heart. Thou wilt not take into thy heart my law, which tells thee, Be merciful as I am merciful. Then thou shalt feel another and an equally universal law of mine. As thou doest so shalt thou be done by. If thou art merciful, thou shalt find mercy. If thou wilt have nothing but retribution, then nothing but retribution thou shalt have. If thou must needs do justice thyself, I will do justice likewise. Because I am merciful, dost thou think me careless? Because I sit still, that I am patient? Dost thou think me such a one as thyself?' And his lord delivered him to the tormentors till he should pay all that was due unto him.

My dear friends, this is an awful story. Let us lay it to heart. And to do that, let us pray God to lay it to our hearts; to write His laws in our hearts, that we may not only fear them, but love them; not only see their profitableness, but their fitness; that we may obey them, not grudgingly or of necessity, but obey them because they look to us just, and true, and beautiful, and as they are—Godlike. Let us pray, I say, that God would make us love what He commands, lest we should neglect and despise what He commands, and find it some day unexpectedly alive and terrible after all. Let us pray to God to keep alive His kingdom of grace within us, lest His kingdom of retribution outside us should fall upon us, and grind us to powder.

SERMON XIX.

CIVILIZED BARBARISM.

(Preached for the Bishop of London's Fund, at St. John's Church, Notting Hill, June 1866.)

ST. MATTHEW ix. 12.

They that be whole need not a physician, but they that are sick.

I HAVE been honoured by an invitation to preach on behalf of the Bishop of London's Fund for providing for the spiritual wants of this metropolis. By the bishop, and a large number of landowners, employers of labour, and others who were aware of the increasing heathendom of the richest and happiest city of the world, it was agreed that, if possible, a million sterling should be raised during the next ten years, to do what money could do in wiping out this national disgrace. It is a noble plan ; and it has been as yet— and I doubt not will be to the end—nobly responded to by the rich laity of this metropolis.

More than 100,000*l.* was contributed during the first six months; nearly 60,000*l.* in the ensuing year ; beside subscriptions which are promised for the whole, or part of the ten years. The money, therefore, does not flow in as rapidly as was desired: but there is as yet no falling off. And I believe that there will be, on the contrary, a gradual increase in the subscriptions as the objects of this fund are better understood, and as its benefits are practically felt.

Now, it is unnecessary—it would be almost an impertinence—to enlarge on a spiritual destitution of which you are already well aware. There are, we shall all agree, many thousands in London who are palpably sick of spiritual disease, and need the physician. But I have special reasons for not pressing this point. If I attempted to draw subscriptions from you by painting tragical and revolting pictures of the vice, heathendom, and misery of this metropolis, I might make you fancy that it was an altogether vicious, heathen, and miserable spot: than which there can be no greater mistake. These evils are not the rule, but the exceptions. Were they not the exceptions, then not merely the society of London, and the industry of London, and the wealth of London, but the very buildings of London, the brick and the mortar, would crumble to the ground by natural and inevitable decay. The unprecedentedly rapid increase of London is, I firmly believe, a sure sign that things in it are done on the whole not ill, but well; that God's blessing is on the place; that, because it is on the whole obeying the eternal laws of God, therefore it is increasing, and multiplying, and replenishing the earth, and subduing it. And I do not hesitate to say, that I have read of no spot of like size upon this earth, on which there have ever been congregated so many human beings, who are getting their bread so peaceably, happily, loyally, and virtuously; and doing their duty— ill enough, no doubt, as we all do it—but still doing it more or less, by man and God.

I am well aware that many will differ from me; that many men and many women—holy, devoted, spending their lives in noble and unselfish labours—persons whose shoes' latchet I am not worthy to unloose—take a far darker view of the state of this metropolis. But the fact is, that they are naturally brought in contact chiefly with its darker side. Their first duty is to seek out cases of misery: and even if they do not, the miserable will, of their own accord, come to them. It is their first duty too—if they be clergymen—to rebuke, and if possible, to cure, open vice, open heathendom, as well as to relieve present want and wretchedness: and may God's blessing be on all who do that work. But in doing it they are dealing daily—and ought to deal, and must deal—with the exceptional, and not with the normal; with cases of palpable and shocking disease, and not with cases of at least seeming health. They see that, into London, as into a vast sewer, gravitates yearly all manner of vice, ignorance, weakness, poverty: but they are apt to forget, at times—and God knows I do not blame them for it in the least—that there gravitates into London, not as into a sewer, but as into a wholesome and fruitful garden, a far greater amount of health, strength, intellect, honesty, industry, virtue, which makes London; which composes, I verily believe, four-fifths of the population of London. For if it did not, as I have said already, London would decay and die, and not grow and live.

Am I denying the spiritual destitution of this metropolis? Am I arguing against the necessity of the Bishop of London's Fund? Am I trying to cool your generosity towards it? Am I raising against it the text —'They that be whole need not a physician, but they that are sick?' Am I trying to prove that the sick are fewer than was fancied, the healthy more numerous; and, therefore, the physician less needed? Would to heaven that I dare so do. Would to heaven that I could prove this fund unnecessary and superfluous. But instead thereof, I fear that I must say—that the average of that health, strength, intellect, honesty, industry, virtue, which makes London—that the average of all that, I verily believe, is to be counted (though it knows it not) among the sick, and not among the sound. It is sick, over and above those personal sins which are common to all classes; it is sick of a great social disease; of a disease which is very dangerous for the nation to which we belong; which will increase more and more, and become more and more dangerous, unless it is stopped wholesale, by some such wholesale measure as this. That disease is (paradoxical as it may seem) Want of Civilization; Barbarism, which is the child of ungodliness. And that can, I verily believe again, be cured only (as far as we in the nineteenth century have discovered) by an extension of the parochial system.

And yet—let us beware of that expression—Parochial System. It seems to imply that the parish is a mere system; an artificial arrangement of man's invention. Now that is just what the parish is not. It is founded on local ties; and they are not a system, but a fact. You do not assemble men into parishes: you find them already assembled by fact, which is the will of God. You take your stand upon the merest physical ground of their living next door to each other; their being likely to witness each other's sayings and doings; to help each other and like each other, or to debauch each other and hate each other; upon the fact that their children play in the same street, and teach each other harm or good, thereby influencing generations yet unborn; upon the fact that if one takes cholera or fever, the man who lives next door is liable to take it too—in short, on the broad fact that they are members of each other, for good or evil. You take your stand on this physical ground of mere neighbourhood; and say—This bond of neighbourhood is, after all, one of the most human—yea, of the most Divine—of all bonds. Every man you meet is your brother, and must be, for good or evil: you cannot live without him; you must help, or you must injure, each other. And, therefore, you must choose whether you will be a horde of isolated barbarians—your living in brick and mortar, instead of huts and tents, being a mere accident—barbarians, I say, at continual war with each other: or whether you will go on to become civilized men; that is, fellow-citizens, members of the same body, confessing and exercising duties to each other which are not self-chosen, not self-invented, but real; which encompass you whether you know them or not; laid on you by Almighty God, by the mere fact of your being men and women living in contact with each other.

Out of this great and true law arises the idea of a parish, a local self-government for many civil purposes, as well as ecclesiastical ones, under a priest who—if he is to be considered as a little constitutional monarch—has his powers limited carefully both by the supreme law, by his assessors the church-wardens, and by the democratic constitution of the parish — influences which he is bound, both by law and by Christianity, to obey.

Arising, in the first place, from the fact that our forefathers colonized England in small separate families, each with its own jurisdiction and worship; our country parish churches being, to this day, often the sites of old heathen tribe-temples, and this very place, Notting-hill, being possibly a little colony of the Nottingas—the same tribe which gave their name to the great city of Nottingham; arising from this fact, and from the very ancient institution of frank-pledge between local neighbours, this parochial system, above all other English institutions, has helped to teach us how to govern, and therefore how to civilize, ourselves. It was overlaid, all but extinguished, by the monastic system, during the latter part of the Middle Ages. It re-asserted itself, in fuller vigour than ever, at the Reformation. But with its benefits, its defects were restored likewise. The tendency of the mediæval Church had been to become merely a church for paupers. The tendency of the Church of England during the sixteenth, seventeenth, and eighteenth centuries, was to become merely a church for burghers. It has been, of late, to become merely a church for paupers again. The causes of this reaction are simple enough. Population increased so rapidly that the old parish bounds were broken up; the old parish staff became too small for working purposes. The Church had (and, alas! has still) to be again a missionary church, as she became in the twelfth and thirteenth centuries, when feudal violence had destroyed the self-government of the parishes—often the parishes themselves—and filled the land with pauperism and barbarism. But that is but a transitional state. Her duty is now becoming more and more (and those who wish her well must help her to fulfil her duty) to reorganize the ancient parochial system on a deeper and sounder footing than ever; on a footing which will ensure her being a church, not merely for pauper, nor merely for burgher, but for pauper and for burgher equally and alike.

But some will say that parochial civilization is only a peculiar form of civilization, because its centre is a church. Peculiar? That is the last word which any one would apply to such a civilization, if he knows history. Will any one mention any civilization, past or present, whose centre has not been (as long as it has been living and progressive) a church? All past civilizations—whether heathen or Mussulman, Jew or Christian—have each and every one of them, as a fact, held that the common and local worship of a God was a sign to them of their common and local unity; a sign to them of their religion, that is, the duties which bound them to each other, whether they liked or not. To all races and nations, as yet, their sacred grove, church, temple, or other place of worship, has been a sign to them that their unity and duties were not invented by themselves, but were the will and command of an unseen Being, who would reward or punish them according as they did those duties or left them undone. So it has been in the civilizations of the past. So it will be in the civilization of the future. If the Christian religion were swept away—as it never will be, for it is eternal—and a civilization founded on what is called Nature put in its place, then we should see a worship of something called Nature, and a temple thereof, set up as the symbol of that Natural civilization. So the Jacobins of France—when they tried to civilize France on the mere ground of what they called Reason—had, whether they liked it or not, to instal a worship of Reason, and a goddess of Reason, for as long as they could contrive to last.

To the world's end, a church of some kind or other will be the centre and symbol of every civilization which is worthy of the name; of every civilization which signifies, not merely that men live in somewhat better houses, travel rather faster by railway, and read a few more books (which is the popular meaning of civilization), but which means—as it meant among the Greeks, the Romans, the Jews, the Christians, among those who discovered the idea and the very words which express it—that each and every truly civilized man is a civis, a citizen, the conscious and obedient member of a corporate body which he did not make, but which (in as far as he is not a savage) has made him.

How far from this idea are the great masses of our really wealthy and well-to-do Londoners? How much is it needed, that wise men should try to re-awaken in them the sense of corporate life, and literally civilize them once more!

Consider the case, not of the average wretched, but of the average comfortable man. The small shop-keeper, the workman, skilled or unskilled—how small a consciousness has he of citizenship. What few incentives to regard civism as a solemn duty. For consider, of what is he a member?

He is a member of a family; and, in general, he fulfils his family duties well.

Yes, thank God, the family life of Englishmen is sound. The hearts of the children do not need to be turned to their fathers, or the hearts of the fathers to the children, as they did in Judea of old. Family life, which is the foundation of all national life—nay, of all Christian and church life—is, on the whole, sound. And having that foundation we can build on it safely and well, if we be wise.

But of what else is the average Londoner a member? Of a benefit-club, of a trades' union, of a volunteer corps. Each will be a valuable element of education, for it will teach him that self-government, which is the school of all freedom, of all loyalty, of all true civilization.

Or he may be a member of some Nonconformist sect. That, too, will be a valuable element, for it will teach him the solemn fact of his own personality; his direct responsibility to God for his own soul.

And I cannot pass this point of my sermon without expressing my sense of the great work which the Dissenting sects have done, and are doing, for this land (with which the Bishop of London's plan will in no wise interfere), in teaching this one thing, which the Church of England, while trying to carry out her far deeper and higher conception of organization, has often forgotten; that, after all, and before all, and throughout all, each man stands alone, face to face with Almighty God. This idea has helped to give the middle classes of England an independence, a strong, vigorous, sharp-cut personality, which is an invaluable wealth to the nation. God forbid that we should try to weaken it, even for reasons which may seem to some devout and orthodox.

But all these memberships, after all, are only voluntary ones, not involuntary. They are assumed by man himself—the worldly associations on the ground of mutual interest; the spiritual associations on that of identity of opinions. They are not instituted by God, and nature, and fact, whether the man knows of them or not, likes them or not. They are of the nature of clubs, not of citizenship. They are not founded on that human ground which is, by virtue of the Incarnation, the most divine ground of all. And for the many they do not exist. The majority of small shopkeepers, and the majority of labourers too, are members, as far as they are aware, of nothing, unless it be a club at some neighbouring public-house. The old feudal and burgher bonds of the Middle Age, for good or for evil, have perished by natural and necessary decay; and nothing has taken their place. Each man is growing up more and more isolated; tempted to selfishness, to brutal independence; tempted to regard his fellow-men as rivals in the struggle for existence; tempted, in short, to incivism, to a loss of the very soul and marrow of civilization, while the outward results of it remain; and therefore tempted to a loss of patriotism, of the belief that he possesses here something far more precious than his private fortune, or even his family; even a country for which he must sacrifice, if need be, himself. And if that grow to be the general temper of England, or of London, in some great day of the Lord, some crisis of perplexity, want, or danger,—then may the Lord have mercy upon this land; for it will have no mercy on itself: but divided, suspicious, heartless, cynical, unpatriotic, each class, even each family, even each individual man, will run each his own way, minding his own interest or safety; content, like the debased Jews, if he can find the life of his hand; and—

> 'Too happy if, in that dread day,
> His life be given him for a prey.'

Our fathers saw that happen throughout half Europe, at a crisis when, while the outward crust of civilization was still kept up, the life of it, all patriotism, corporate feeling, duty to a common God, and faith in a common Saviour, had rotted out unperceived. At one blow the gay idol fell, and broke; and behold, inside was not a soul, but dust. God grant that we may never see here the same catastrophe, the same disgrace.

Now, one remedy—I do not say the only remedy—there are no such things as panaceas; all spiritual and social diseases are complicated, and their remedies must be complicated likewise—but one remedy, palpable, easy, and useful, whenever and wherever it has been tried, is this—to go to these great masses of brave, honest, industrious, but isolated and uncivilized men, after the method of the Bishop of this diocese, and his fund; and to say to them,—'Of whatever body you are, or are not members, you are members of that human family for which our Lord Jesus Christ was contented to be betrayed, and to suffer death upon the Cross; over which He now liveth and reigneth, with the Father and the Holy Ghost, one God, world without end. You are children of God the Father of spirits, who wills that all should be saved, and come to the knowledge of the truth. You are inheritors— that is, members not by your own will, or the will of any man, but by the will of God who has chosen you to be born in a Christian land of Christian parents— inheritors, I say, of the kingdom of heaven, from your cradles to your graves, and after that, if you will, for ever and ever. Behave as such. Claim your rights; for they are yours already: and not only claim your rights, but confess your duties. Remember that every man, woman, and child in your street is, primâ facie, just as much a member of Christ as you are. Treat them as such; associate yourselves with them as such. Accept the simple physical fact that they live next door to you, as God's will toward you both, and as God's sign to you that you and they are members of the same human and divine family. Enter with them, in that plain form, into the free corporate self-government of a Christian parish. Fear no priestly tyranny; from that danger you are guaranteed by the fact, that the great majority of the promoters of this fund are laymen, of all shades of opinion. You are guaranteed, still further, by the fact, that in the parochial system there can be no tyranny. It is one of the very institutions by which Englishmen have learnt those habits of self-government, which are the admiration of Europe.

'Do, then, the duty which lies nearest you; your duty to the man who lives next door, and to the man who lives in the next street. Do your duty to your parish; that you may learn to do your duty by your country and to all mankind, and prove yourselves thereby civilized men.

'And confess your sins in this matter, if not to us, at least to God. Confess that while you, in your sturdy, comfortable independence, have been fancying yourselves whole and sound, you have been very sick, and need the physician to cure you of the deadly and growing disease of selfish barbarism. Confess that, while you have been priding yourselves on English self-help and independence, you have not deigned to use them for those purposes of common organization, common worship, for which the very savages and heathens have, for ages past, used such freedom as they have had. Confess that, while you have been talking loudly about the rights of humanity, you have neglected too often its duties, and lived as if the people in the same street had no more to do with you than the beasts which perish.

'Confess your sins. We monied men confess ours. We ought to have foreseen the rapid growth of this city. We ought to have planned and laboured more earnestly for its better organization. And we freely offer our money, as a sign of our repentance, to build and establish for you institutions which you cannot afford to establish for yourselves. We excuse you, moreover, in very great part. You have been gathered together so suddenly into these vast new districts, or rather chaos of houses, and you have meanwhile shifted your dwellings so rapidly, and under the pressure of such continual labour, that you have not had time enough to organize yourselves. But we, too, have our excuse. We have actually been trying, at vast expense and labour to ourselves, for the last forty years, to meet your new needs. But you have outgrown all our efforts. Your increase has taken us by surprise. Your prosperity has outrun our goodwill. It shall do so no more. We are ready to do our part in the good work of repentance. We ask you to do yours. You are more able to do it than you ever were: richer, better educated, more acquainted with the blessings of association. We do not come to you as to paupers, merely to help you. We come to you as to free and independent citizens, to teach you to help yourselves, and show yourselves citizens indeed.'

I hope, ay, I believe, that such an appeal as this, made in an honest and liberal spirit, which proves its honesty and liberality by great and generous gifts out of such private wealth as no nation ever had before, will be met by the masses of London, in the same spirit as that in which it has been made.

I am certain of it, if only the ecclesiastical staff employed by this Fund will keep steadfastly in mind what they have to do. True it is, and happily true, that they can do nothing but good. If they confine themselves to the celebration of public worship, to teaching children, to giving the consolations of religion to those with whom want and wretchedness bring them in contact—all that will be gain, clear gain, vast gain. But that, valuable, necessary as it is, will not be sufficient to evoke a full response from the people of London.

But if they will, not leaving the other undone, do yet more; if they will attempt the more difficult, but the equally necessary and more permanent labour—that of attacking the disease of barbarism, not merely in its symptoms, but in its very roots and its causes; if they will recognise the fact, that with the disease there coexists a great deal of sturdy and useful health; if they will have courage and address to face, not merely the non-working, non-earning, and generally non-thinking hundreds, but the working, earning, thinking thousands of each parish; in fact, the men and women who make London what it is; if they will approach them with charity, confidence, and respect; if they will remember that they are justly jealous of that personal independence, that civil and religious liberty, which is theirs by law and right; if they will conduct themselves, not as lords over God's heritage, but as examples to the flock; if they will treat that flock, not as their subjects, but as their friends, their fellow-workers, their fellow-counsellors—often their advisers; if they will remember that 'Give and take, live and let live,' are no mere worldly maxims, but necessary, though difficult Christian duties; then, I believe, they will after awhile receive an answer to their call such as they dare not as yet expect; such an answer as our forefathers gave to the clergy of the early Middle Age, when they showed them that the kingdom of God was the messenger of civilization, of humanity, of justice and peace, of strength and well-being in this world, as well as in the next. The clergy would find in the men and women of London not merely disciples, but helpers. They would meet, not with fanatical excitement, not even with enthusiasm, not even with much outward devotion; but with co-operation, hearty and practical though slow and quiet—co-operation all the more valuable, in every possible sense, because it will be free and voluntary; and the Bishop of London's Fund would receive more and more assistance, not merely of heads and hands, but of money when money was needed, from the inhabitants of the very poorest and most heathen districts, as they began to feel that they were giving their money towards a common blessing, and became proud to pay their share towards an organization which would belong to them, and to their children after them.

So runs my dream. This may be done : God grant that it may ! For now, it may be, is our best chance of doing it. Now is the accepted time ; now is the day of salvation. If these masses increase in numbers and in power for another generation, in their present state of anarchy, they may be lost for ever to Christianity, to order, to civilization. But if we can civilize, in that sense which is both classical and Christian, the masses of London, and of England, by that parochial method which has been (according to history) the only method yet discovered, then we shall have helped, not only to save innumerable souls from sin, and from that misery which is the inevitable and everlasting consequence of sin, but we shall have helped to save them from a specious and tawdry barbarism, such as corrupted and enervated the seemingly civilized masses of the later Roman empire; and to save our country, within the next century, from some such catastrophe as overtook the Jewish monarchy in spite of all its outward religiosity; the catastrophe which has overtaken every nation which has fancied itself sound and whole, while it was really broken, sick, weak, ripe for ruin. For such, every nation or empire becomes, though the minority above be never so well organized, civilized, powerful, educated, even virtuous, if the majority below are not a people of citizens, but masses of incoherent atoms, ready to fall to pieces before every storm.

From that, and from all adversities, may God deliver us, and our children after us, by graciously beholding this His Family, for which our Lord Jesus Christ was content to suffer death upon the Cross; and by pouring out His Spirit upon all estates of men in His holy Church, that every member of the same, in his calling and ministry, may freely and godly serve Him; till we have no longer the shame and sorrow of praying for English men and women, as we do for Jews, Turks, infidels, and heretics, that God would take from them all ignorance, hardness of heart, and contempt of His Word, and fetch them home to that flock of His, to which they all belong!

SERMON XX.

THE GOD OF NATURE.

(Preached during a wet harvest.)

PSALM cxlvii. 7—9.

Sing unto the Lord with thanksgiving; sing praise upon the harp unto our God: who covereth the heaven with clouds, who prepareth rain for the earth, who maketh grass to grow upon the mountains. He giveth to the beast his food, and to the young ravens which cry.

THERE is no reason why those who wrote this Psalm, and the one which follows it, should have looked more cheerfully on the world about them than we have a right to do. The country and climate of Judea is not much superior to ours. If we suffer at times from excess of rain and wind, Judea suffers from excess of drought and sunshine. It suffers, too, at times, from that most terrible of earthly calamities, from which we are free—namely, from earthquakes. The sea, moreover, instead of being loved, as it is by us, as the highway of our commerce, and the producer of vast stores of food—the sea, I say, was almost feared by the old

Jews, who were no sailors. They looked on it as a dangerous waste; and were thankful to God that, though the waves roared, He had set them a bound which they could not pass.

So that there is no reason why the old Jews should think and speak more cheerfully about the world than we here in England ought. They had, too, the same human afflictions, sicknesses, dangers, disappointments, losses and chastisements as we have. They had their full share of all the ills to which flesh is heir. Yet look, I beg you, at the cheerfulness of these two Psalms, the 147th and 148th. In truth, it is more than cheerfulness; it is joy, rejoicing which can only express itself in a song.

These Psalms are songs, to be sung to music, and even in our translation they are songs still, sounding like poetry, and not like prose.

And why is this? Because the men who wrote these Psalms had faith in God.

They trusted God. They saw that He was worthy of their trust. They saw that He was to be honoured, not merely for His boundless wisdom and His boundless power: for a being might have them, and yet make a bad use of them. But He was to be trusted, because He was a good God. He was to be honoured, not for anything which men might get out of Him (as the heathen fancied) by flattering Him, and begging of Him:

but He was to be honoured for His own sake, for what He was in Himself—a just, merciful, kind, generous, magnanimous, and utterly noble and perfect, moral Being, worthy of all admiration, praise, honour, and glory.

The Psalmist saw that God was good, and worthy to be praised. But he saw, too, that he and his forefathers would never have found out that for themselves. It was too great a discovery for man to make. God must have showed it to them. God had showed His word to Jacob, His statutes and ordinances to Israel.

He had not done so to any other nation, neither had the heathen knowledge of His laws. And, therefore, they did not trust God; they did not consider Him a good God, and so they worshipped Baalim, the sun and moon and stars, with silly and foul ceremonies, to procure from them good harvests; and burnt their children in the fire to Moloch, the fire-king, to keep off the earthquakes and the floods. God had not taught them what He had taught Israel—to trust in Him, and in His word which ran very swiftly, and in His laws, which could not be broken: a faith which, my friends, we must do our best to keep up in ourselves, and in our children after us. For it is very easy to lose it, this faith in God. We are tempted to lose it, all our lives long.

Our forefathers, in the days of Popery, lost it; and because they did not trust in God as a good God, who took good care of the world which He had made, they fell to believing that the devil, and witches, the servants of the devil, could raise storms, blight crops, strike cattle and human beings with disease. And they began, too, to pray, not to God, but to certain saints in heaven, to protect them against bodily ills.

One saint could cure one disease, and one another; one saint protected the cattle, another kept off thunder, and so forth—I will not tell you more, lest I should tempt you to smile in this holy place; and tempt you, too, to look down on your forefathers, who (though they made these mistakes) were just as honest and virtuous men as we.

And even lately, up to this very time, there are those who have not full faith in God; though they be good and pious persons, and good Protestants too, who would shrink with horror from worshipping saints, or any being save God alone. But they are apt to shut their eyes to the beauty and order of God's world, and to the glory of God set forth therein, and to excuse themselves by quoting unfairly texts of Scripture. They say that this world is all out of joint; corrupt, and cursed for Adam's sin: yet, where it is out of joint, and where it is corrupt, they cannot show. And, as for its being cursed for Adam's sin, that is a dream which is contradicted by Holy Scripture itself. For see. We read in Genesis iii. 17, 'Cursed is the ground for thy sake; in sorrow shalt thou eat of it all the days of thy life; thorns also and thistles shall it bring forth to thee.'

Now, that the ground does not now bring forth thorns and thistles to us, we know. For it brings forth whatsoever fair flower, or useful herb, we plant therein, according to the laws of nature, which are the laws of God. Neither do men eat thereof in sorrow; but, as Solomon says, 'eat their bread in joyfulness of heart.' And so did they in the Psalmist's days; who never speak of the tillage of the land without some expression of faith and confidence, and thankfulness to that God who crowns the year with His goodness, and His clouds drop fatness; while the hills rejoice on every side, and the valleys stand so thick with corn, that they laugh and sing—of faith, I say, and gratitude toward that God who brings forth the grass for the cattle, and green herb for the service of men; who brings food out of the earth, and wine to make glad the heart of man, and oil to give him a cheerful countenance, and bread to strengthen man's heart. Those well-known words are in the 104th Psalm; and I ask any reasonable person to read that Psalm through—the Psalm which contains the Jewish natural theology, the Jew's view of this world, and of God's will and dealings with it — and then say, could a man have written it who thought that there was any curse upon this earth on account of man's sin?

But more. The Book of Genesis says that there is none; for, after it has said in the third chapter, 'Cursed is the ground for thy sake,' it says again, in the eighth chapter, verse 21, 'And the Lord said in His heart, I will not again curse the ground for man's sake. While the earth remaineth, seed-time and harvest, cold and heat, summer and winter, shall not cease.'

Can any words be plainer? Whatever the curse in Adam's days may have been, does not the Book of Genesis represent it as being formally abrogated and taken away in the days of Noah, that the regular course of nature, fruitful and beneficent, might endure thenceforth?

Accordingly, we hear no more in the Bible anywhere of this same curse. We hear instead the very opposite; for one says, in the 119th Psalm, speaking indeed of God, 'O Lord, Thy word endureth for ever in heaven. Thy truth also remaineth from one generation to another. Thou hast laid the foundation of the earth, and it abideth. They continue this day according to Thine ordinance: for all things serve Thee.' And so in the 148th Psalm, another speaks by the Spirit of God; 'Let all things praise the name of the Lord: for He commanded, and they were created. He hath also established them for ever and ever: He hath given them a law which shall not be broken.'

Yes, my friends, God's law shall not be broken, and it is not broken. And that faith, that the laws which govern the whole material universe, cannot be broken, will be to us faith full of hope, and joy, and confidence, if we will remember, with the Psalmist, that they are the laws of the living God, and of the good God.

They are the laws of the living God: not the laws of nature, or fate, or necessity—all three words which mean little or nothing—but of a living God in whom we live, and move, and have our being; whose word— the creating, organizing, inspiring word—runneth very swiftly, making all things to obey God, and not themselves.

And they are the laws of a good God; of a moral God; of a generous, loving, just, and merciful God, who, as the Psalmist reminds us (and that is the reason of his confidence and his joy), while He telleth the number of the stars, and calleth them all by their names, condescends at the same time to heal those who are broken in heart; of a God who, while He giveth fodder to the cattle, and feedeth the young ravens who call on Him, at the same time careth for those who fear Him, and put their trust in His mercy; of a God who, while His power is great and His wisdom infinite, at the same time sets up the meek, and brings the ungodly down to the ground; of a Father in heaven who is perfect in this—that He sends His sun and rain alike on the just and the unjust, and is good to the unthankful and the evil; of a Father, lastly, who so loved the world, that He spared not His only-begotten Son, but freely gave Him for us, and has committed to that Son all power in heaven and earth;—all power over the material world, which we call nature, as well as over the moral world, which is the hearts and spirits of men—to that Word of God who runneth very swiftly, who is sharper than a two-edged sword, and yet more tender than the love of woman; even Jesus Christ the Saviour, the Word of God, who was in the beginning with God, and was God; by whom all things were made; who is the true Light, which lighteth every man that cometh into the world, if by any means he will receive the light of God, and see thereby the true and wise laws of Nature and of Spirit.

This is our God. This is He who sends food and wealth, rain and sunshine. Shall we not trust Him? If we thank Him for plenty, and fine weather, which we see to be blessings without doubt, shall we not trust Him for scarcity and bad weather, which do not seem to us to be blessings, and yet may be blessings nevertheless? Shall we not believe that His very chastisements are mercies? Shall we not accept them in faith, as the child takes from its parent's hand bitter medicine, the use of which it cannot see; but takes it in faith that its parent knows best, and that its parent's purpose is only love and benevolence? Shall we not say with Job—Though He slay me, yet will I trust in Him? He cannot mean my harm; He must mean my good, and the good of all mankind. He must—even by such seeming calamities as great rains, or failure of crops—even by them He must be benefiting mankind. Recollect, as a single instance, that the great rains of 1860, which terrified so many, are proved now to have saved some thousands of lives in England from fever and similar diseases. Take courage; and have, as the old Psalmist had, faith in God. Believe that nothing goes wrong in this world, save through the sin, and folly, and ignorance of man; that God is always right, always wise, always benevolent: and be sure that you, each and all, are—

> 'Safe in the hand of one disposing Power,
> Or in the natal, or the mortal hour,
> All nature is but art, unknown to thee;
> All chance, discretion which thou cans' not see.
> All discord, harmony not understood;
> All partial evil, universal good;
> And spite of pride, in erring reason's spite,
> One truth is clear—whatever is, is right.'

And pray to God that He may fill you with His Spirit, the spirit of wisdom and understanding, of knowledge and grace of the Lord, and show to you, as He showed to the Jews of old, His laws and judgments, and so teach you how to see that the only thing on earth which is not right, is—the sin of man.

www.ingramcontent.com/pod-product-compliance
Lightning Source LLC
Chambersburg PA
CBHW031730230426
43669CB00007B/304